INSPIRATIONAL PRESENCE

The Art of Transformational Leadership

JEFF EVANS, PH.D.

New York

Inspirational Presence
The Art of Transformational Leadership

Softcover ISBN: 978-1-60037-570-5
Hardcover ISBN: 978-1-60037-571-2

Library of Congress Control Number: 2009921176

MORGAN · JAMES
THE ENTREPRENEURIAL PUBLISHER

Morgan James Publishing, LLC
1225 Franklin Ave., STE 325
Garden City, NY 11530-1693
Toll Free 800-485-4943
www.MorganJamesPublishing.com

In an effort to support local communities, raise awareness and funds, Morgan James Publishing donates one percent of all book sales for the life of each book to Habitat for Humanity. Get involved today, visit **www.HelpHabitatForHumanity.org**.

PREFACE

Why this book, and why now? Our world is one of expanding economies and increasing global impact and awareness. This web of connectedness demands a new leadership style and a new type of leadership consciousness. Current research on emotional intelligence and intention affirms the importance of emotionally literate and globally aware people. While we live in countries organized as nations, the preponderance of global companies is expanding past national boundaries, past economic systems, and past cultural norms. Leaders in these organizations are explorers in a world of connections yet to be discovered.

The pioneers in this emerging world will be forced to lead from a place of global and enterprise thinking. They will have to rely on people with whom they do not relate culturally, who live halfway around the world, who move in different time zones, observe different holidays, pray to different gods, follow different laws and customs, and who even have different economic values and principles. Yet in spite of those differences, they all must share a common sense of direction, purpose, and global identity. They must experience a connectedness that transcends these differences. In this world, the rule-based leadership in use for the last hundred years or so is becoming less and less relevant.

These leaders must be far more comfortable with ambiguity and with leading through influence. These leaders must be fluent in the language of humanity, in the universal connections of heart and spirit. They must connect through rapport rather than positional power. These leaders must understand the art of inspiration, which breaks the reliance on motivation used for so long in Western culture. These leaders must understand systems and organizations, rather than organization charts and policies. These leaders must start now.

The skills of inspiration and influence are innate to humans and have been known for millennia. Leaders have used these skills to create change in many settings throughout our recorded history. The issue now has to do with the relative importance of these skills. The magnitude of interpersonal connections being created globally is at a point never before experienced in human history. Our planet is on the verge of massive change that demands global thinking. Even though our focus is on the corporate setting, the main objective is to create leaders who can connect around the world. These leaders must be able to create new perspectives, new thinking, and inspire people to take action in different directions—because people want to, not because they have to.

For example, look at global warming. This issue must be solved by people who are working from a consistent level of global thinking and looking at this issue from a much larger context than ever before. Einstein said: "We cannot solve our problems with the same thinking we used when we created them." Global warming is clearly a case where the limited thinking of past generations created a set of problems that can be solved only by a new way of thinking—and this is only one issue on which we could focus. There are many such issues, and we intuitively know that some of them have not yet come to our attention. We know that a new generation of global leaders must step into the space of creating transformation in our world.

This book is an outgrowth of ongoing action research done through our consulting firm, which specializes in developing unique and powerful leadership in global settings. As such, it is a reflection of grounded theory in action, where the user can take what we have learned and apply it in his or her work, community, and personal life. Our practice has, through the years, used a meta-model, bringing in the work of emotional intelligence (Goleman et al), leadership models (Posner & Kouzes, Hertzberger, others), and systems thinking (various Gestalt theorists and systems scientists). As we have done successfully with our work in the *Ten Tasks of Change* (Evans & Schaefer, 2001), we have allowed the theory to stay in the background and directed the focus on how it is used. After years of working through large-scale organizational change, it seemed that the focus was consistently on the leaders and how they transformed themselves in order to transform the organization. This work is a culmination of this practice and is published with the intent of sharing what gets results.

Inspirational Presence was written for people who want to embody these changes and be the forces for change in the world. Although there are thousands of research studies available that document many aspects of leadership and transformation, it is the work of other volumes to present that information. The work of this book is to teach leaders *how* they can accomplish transformation in the simplest form possible. My highest aspiration for this book is simply for it to be useful. I hope it will open a way of thinking for people who want to transform their environments and provide a guide that will fuel positive and creative change in the world.

ACKNOWLEDGMENTS

I have spent a lifetime in a mode of learning and experimentation, with teachers being as many and as varied as you can imagine. My background is a mosaic, earning degrees in literature and history before degrees in human development. Along the line, however, there have been many people who have left a profound impact on the way I move in the world. Some are long gone, and their impact has transcended time and distance. During the course of my life, I have read many books, all of which have contributed some part of the way that I see the world; of those, I will mention a few.

Early in life I was blessed to read the great works of Voltaire, Nietzsche, Payne, and others who profoundly impacted what I thought of democracy and human equality. Together, these set me on a path that embodies many egalitarian values. Among those, Ralph Waldo Emerson had the most memorable and lasting impact. I reread his works when I turned thirty-eight, as that was his age when he was in the prime of his writing. That was a humbling experience. Mark Twain showed me the ability to connect culture and feeling through words and sly humor. His characters leapt off the pages and still had relevance one hundred years after he penned them.

More recently, there are a number of gifted and inspiring authors who have made a huge difference for me. Gary Zukav has written works that have been turning points for me. First, *The Dancing Wu Li Masters*; then, more recently, *The Heart of the Soul*. Peter Senge's *The Fifth Discipline* was another pivotal point in my learning progression. Ken Wilber's *A Brief History of Everything* and *The Marriage of Sense and Soul* gave me insight into integration. Many other fine authors, researchers, and theorists have contributed to my cognitive worldview and, therefore, greatly influenced the content of this book.

Then there are those who have been my teachers in action. They have shown me ways to work with human consciousness in deep and powerful ways: John Carter at the Gestalt Institute of Cleveland, who showed me how spiritual practices and working with leaders can be the same thing. Tim Hallbom of NLP California, who taught me (and many others) how to create instant change through our language and thinking. My friend and colleague Chuck Schaefer, who brought me into the professional community of organization development, taught me many concepts of high-performance work systems, and expanded my thinking on many of my projects.

I owe a special thanks to my dad, Dan Evans, who showed me what it was like to be passionate about learning, and to my mother, Patricia Evans, who in her deep passion for writing, taught me to always carry a pen and paper, as I never knew when I would feel like I really needed to write.

Most of all, I owe thanks to my beloved wife, Justina Vail Evans. She is a gifted artist, writer, actor, spiritual teacher, and coach who has loved me, taught me, and learned with me. Justina has prompted my thinking, read my drafts, and provided valuable insights to the concepts, content, and presentation of this work. She has taught me the meaning of inspiration and embodies the example of presence. It is only through her that this book has been written.

CONTENTS

INTRODUCTION

When you pray, move your feet.

—Native American saying

There is a little known reality associated with the skills of leadership. As a leader's sphere of influence increases, the requirement for skills related to emotional intelligence goes up as well. In fact, as much as 90 percent of leader success can be attributed to these skills (Goleman, 2003). Along with that reality comes an associated challenge. That is, it can be difficult for leaders to see or accept this shift. There is a simple reason for this challenge, and it has nothing to do with leaders being slow, dumb, or incompetent. On the contrary, it has to do with people being quick, smart, and competent. The entry point for most organizations requires a high competency in technical ability. Success, as it relates to job mobility and promotions, comes early from using this, which becomes a self-validating reality. This is also true in educational settings. Success comes from what you did last, not where you are going next. However, predicting future success from the use of these technical abilities is like driving by looking in the rearview mirror. It doesn't tell what will create success where you are going.

To further compound this, these transition points for leaders are rarely taught from the perspective of requiring new levels of relationship skills. A natural progression of leadership, without a conscious change in path, would have a leader continually attempting to lead from technically based strategies that served in the past but no longer serve the current situation without a support network or guide to show a new path. Growing into leadership requires courage, as the new challenges of expanded influence require new and often untested approaches for the leader. This overall generalization led to Laurence Peter's book *The Peter Principle*, in which his premise was that in a hierarchy each employee rises to his or her personal level of incompetency. While this has been used by various people as either a joke or a fact, there is an element of truth within the premise. It can be true of how hierarchies function, but it does not represent an absolute truth about human ability. It is simply a perspective of human development that recognizes the need to use different skills as the situation changes, and these skills are often not obvious to the leaders who need them.

LEADERSHIP FROM THE INSIDE OUT

The skills and approaches that will guide leaders through a journey of expanded influence are known and learnable. These aspects can be found in the research on high-performing organizations and the research on neuroscience. This research is now becoming clear with regard to how a leader's engagement style can be quantified through performance measures. While there are many correlates to success in emotional intelligence for leaders, we start with two fundamental differences in approach.

The first perspective is one of self-preservation. This makes a leader conservative and cautious. The primary aspects you will see from this perspective are related to control and predictability. These leaders want to be able to repeatedly and reliably replicate the past and thereby produce stability. The strategies at play with this perspective tend to be slow to change and quite risk-averse.

Second, we can operate from a perspective of self-realization. Leaders in this mode are far more experimental and innovative. These leaders tend to become skeptical of previously used strategies and tend to want to leverage them into new ways of operating or achieving new goals. These leaders are change-ready and willing to take risks. They tend to not feel a strong linkage to or need for authority, and they tend to question the value of stability.

In *The Heart of the Soul*, Gary Zuckav brings this down to much simpler terms. He states (and I firmly believe) that we are, at all times, either acting from "love and trust" (self-realization) or "fear and doubt" (self-preservation). This is probably the most basic component of our work. Through this, we work with inspiration, helping leaders connect to the deeper parts of themselves. From there, we take action on that inspiration, in an intentional and connected way. This work will help leaders understand those callings and teach them how to move those ideas into action in ways that support large-scale organization change.

This book will deal with the leader on an individual level as well as larger levels of the system, such as a team or an organization. I started in this field, working with large groups of people as an organization-change consultant, hence my first work on large scale change, *Ten Tasks of Change*. During the years of consulting work, I spent most of my time teaching leaders how to change an organization by first changing themselves. This is the biggest differentiator of *Inspirational Presence* in that it teaches leaders how to effect change across many layers of organization through transformational change.

Consequently, there are many references in this book to *change*, which might seem odd when you think of it as a book on leadership. In truth, leadership and change are tied tightly together, as you rarely lead people to where they already are. New undertakings and directions are achieved when people see the world in new ways and spend their days doing different things. Therefore, it is critical to understand the aspects of how people engage new concepts and how a leader can influence this.

OVERVIEW

Inspirational Presence presents a framework of what makes a leader and what makes that leader powerful and able to support transformation. The book focuses on transformational change or when the rules of engagement change. This is the sort of change that brings about reform movements and restructures businesses. Transformational change creates new paradigms about what is possible in the world of business as well as humanity.

In this book you will encounter the use of the word *spirit*—it is not meant to be religious but to denote the connection of human spirit and our perpetual desire to be more, to be connected to a higher source or a greater cause, and a yearning to make a deep and lasting impact on the planet in the years we spend here. In the early years of my work in organization development, a colleague told me that most people who spent any amount of time in this field wound up on some sort of spiritual journey through self-exploration. My experience has shown that statement to be true and, if anything, a bit limited. In my studies of literature and history, I tend to see a much more expanded view of that and believe that every human on this planet goes through some sort of spiritual quest in his or her life. Some are deeper than others, some are longer, and some are more life-encompassing than others. At any rate, it is part of being human. We all hold in our core this spiritual being that is connected at much higher levels of consciousness than we realize most of the time.

Inspirational Presence is about connecting with that spirit, but it is not necessarily about the quest itself. This book is about what to do with that energy and how to create a world in which those aspirations can manifest. The passion of that direction becomes the energy of creativity and a connection that drives us and fuels us. It is what sustains us when we might otherwise feel all alone in the world, particularly when we are off the beaten path, forging new directions, leading the wave of innovation, or just standing up for something simply because it matters.

Throughout time, cultures and religions have believed and lived out practices that held a time in our lives for a spiritual awakening; a time when we became aware of a higher purpose or a deep calling within us to do more than exist from day to day. In more recent times, this seems to have become more routine than meaningful, so we often have to look for other means of awakening that spirit with us.

This book is written from a belief that we can find that spirit through fairly simple means, as it is always there and always accessible. We simply need to listen. Our beings are perfectly designed to operate from a higher level of consciousness, and it is not something that we have to learn. There may be practices from our ego and our humanity that we need to unlearn that can get in the way of the essence of our being, but those will become clear as we listen. For now, let us just believe that those things will unfold.

The principles put forth here are a synthesis of practices and research in the areas of leadership, systems theory, psychology, emotional intelligence, and consciousness. They are meant to be a guide for meaningful action. The practices themselves are simply mechanisms through which you can access the power of leadership from within yourself and put it forth into the world in a manner that people can easily join. The practices apply to any endeavor and seem to be cross-culturally applicable.

HOW TO USE THIS BOOK

This book is a guidebook, intended to present concepts and practical ways to use them. Think of it as a reference guide to your leadership development. Each chapter presents a concept that stands for a critical piece of the leadership equation. Each can stand alone and, when studied and adopted, will significantly improve your ability to lead. Put together, the chapters form an integrated framework through which you can learn to create and sustain profound change in others. There are a number of competencies presented, and it is intended to be simple.

It is most valuable to allow yourself the latitude of thinking how this book may present concepts in a different way from those you have heard before. Look for the simplicity here and the elegance that you can achieve as a leader, simply by applying a few principles and practicing some simple techniques.

One of the principles of change that has been a centerpiece of our work is that change can occur quite easily. All we have to do is change our minds. Once we see the world in a different way and look for different data, we immediately create new realities. The only things left are ordering all the mechanical aspects of our lives to align with our new way of thinking.

The issues we have found in our years of working through personal and organizational change are not lack of good ideas or desire of people to create different conditions; they have been the strength of organization designs and management systems that intentionally and reliably function to perpetuate the current state. The effort involved in change is one of constantly disconnecting from old ways and connecting with new, with as much integrity and conviction as we can muster.

Our world and our systems need transformation, and we need leaders to do this. With the size of the systems that we now have in play, we need many, many leaders who are operating at all levels to make these changes. We need world leaders who will take on the transformational aspects of nations and international issues. We need leaders who will lead schools and communities to create more than has previously been imagined. We need business leaders who will create emerging business models that are created holistically and generate collateral good to communities and their environment.

Whatever sort of leader you are, use this guide to enhance your ability to create transformation. Start with yourself, then your sphere of influence, and then increasingly increase your scope. Today, you; tomorrow, the world.

CHAPTER 1—
THE CASE FOR INSPIRATION

Our chief want is someone who will inspire
us to be what we know we could be.

—Ralph Waldo Emerson

Buddha. Jesus. Mohammed. Mahatma Gandhi. Nelson Mandela. Aung San Suu Kyi. His Holiness the Dalai Lama. John F. Kennedy. Indira Gandhi. Sequoyah. Abraham Lincoln. Sir Winston Churchill. Eleanor Roosevelt. Desmond Tutu. Maya Angelou. Mikhail Gorbachev. Dr. Martin Luther King, Jr. Oprah Winfrey. Al Gore. Jeremy Gilley.

What do they all have in common?

Each of those people is known for the difference he or she made in the world. They made contributions through their ability to follow a passion and inspire others with their commitment and connection with people. They were clear and engaging with others. While in every case, there were people who did not agree with them or did not follow their lead, there also were plenty who did. They have each made big differences in the world. In every case, they can inspire us to become more of who we truly know we could be. Their passion can ignite ours.

There are also other leaders—each of us can name someone—who have made differences through the expression of personal passion and their ability to engage others in their direction. I can think of a small number of teachers and people in industry who stand out for me as having been real leaders in their sphere of influence. I would bet that you can, too. You probably had the teacher whom you fondly remember because of how you were changed forever by him or her at a critical point in life. Or maybe you remember the one boss who truly had purpose and connection, who inspired you to achieve. I know I can.

The moment that these special people opened themselves to the world and allowed others access to their passions and purpose, they became leaders. When we engaged their connection with humanity, we experienced a personal transformation. Through that contact, our world was irreversibly changed. Those people remain in our minds because of the impact they had on each of us as a person. We can still feel the emotions associated with them. We remember the experience of being with them. They had inspirational presence. So can you.

INSPIRATIONAL PRESENCE

Presence is that portion of another human being that you sense without consciously trying to do so. This presence can be small or large, compelling or repelling, indefinite yet palpable; it is the basis of connection between human beings. Each of us has presence, and that presence can be sensed by others around us. We do find, however, that some people have a presence that is more noticeable than others and often more compelling than others. Some are noticeable when they walk into a room. Others we notice when they get close to us. Some, we barely notice at all.

Presence, by itself, can be either positive or negative in its effect on others. We have all been around people who make our skin crawl for no apparent reason. We have been around people who make us nervous. We have also been around people who make us laugh or just feel good. Each of these has a different presence, big enough to influence our own state of being. But how does that presence relate to an ability to lead? Once people notice our presence, what does it take to have them want to move in the direction we are going, to buy in to our passion, and to commit their energy to our path?

When we become inspired, our presence becomes more pronounced. Our energy field gets stronger, and our impact on others is more positive. It feels better to be around inspired people than around people who are not. There is smoothness to their energy that compels us to stop, take notice, and listen. To begin to influence others at a personal level, we must have a connection with our own humanity and purpose and allow that connection to be accessed by others. We need a presence that is powerful and compelling. This is obtained through emotional availability and the resonance of a passionate purpose. Along with this purpose comes the optimism, enthusiasm, and self-confidence to pursue it. Then we can open ourselves and learn the transparency and authenticity that allows others to know us, to know what is important to us, and to connect with us around our passion.

Inspirational presence is the ability to connect authentically with others; to use our thoughts, feelings, and intuitions to guide action toward our deepest sense of personal mission.

INSPIRATION VS. MOTIVATION

Inspiration is a word that is used in many areas and in many contexts, but it's not that often associated with leadership. Motivation is a more commonly used word when referring to leadership and management roles. Each of you will have your own preliminary definition or association with inspiration and probably can recall times when you found a person or an event or even a sunset particularly inspiring. We all know the feeling of being inspired and the many and varied ways that the word is used. For this book and this model, however, we want to condense it to a specific definition and a particular usage.

Let us start our exploration of the difference between the energy of inspiration and the energy of motivation with some definitions. The main entry for *inspiration* in the dictionary is "ecstasy," which means to "stand outside the ordinary self." Synonyms for inspiration are blessedness, bliss, delight, delirium, ebullience, elation, enthusiasm, exaltation, fervor, gladness, happiness, joy, and rapture. The main entry for *motivation* is "excitement." Its synonyms are action, activity, ado, agitation, drama, enthusiasm, excitation, fever, flurry, furor, movement, stimulation, turmoil, and wildness. These are very different words that describe widely dissimilar emotional states. We can see that inspiration has connotations that allow us to be still within ourselves and in an inspired place. Motivation, with its orientation toward action, is more what we experience when we are bursting with energy and can't wait to do something.

Most of us have experienced the meeting or event that is filled with motivational techniques. We get the bright lights, the loud music, the cheering from the stage. Invariably, these events will have us on our feet, clapping and making plenty of notes about what we will do next. These events can find resonance within us and spur us to action. This sort of energy definitely has its place. It jars us out of our seats, out of our comfort zone, and it charges our adrenaline. It has us making lists and setting goals. This is the key scene of so many feel-good movies, in which we see the rousing and moving half-time speech in the locker room of the big game. It is the speech that stirs our blood, bringing tears to our eyes and power to our limbs, leaving us pulsing with vitality and a renewed sense of determination and purpose. We breathe more freely, and our thoughts are focused. This is the energy of motivation that gets athletes to turn the game around in the critical second half.

But what about the other times? What about the early mornings when no one else is around? What about the quiet places in the day when we are looking for something else or the next place to direct our attention and energy? These times call for inspiration, drawn from deep within ourselves. It is the energy that we pull up from our deepest, most connected places. It sustains us through good times as well as adversity. We find it possible to be motivated without inspiration following. It is impossible, however, to be inspired without its being followed by motivation. To be truly inspired demands action.

We can take an even deeper meaning of inspiration—that it is the divine breath of life. For our purposes, we need leaders who understand their connection to causes greater than themselves. We need leaders who can connect with the people around them in deep and profound ways, coupling the drive of human passion with the wisdom and intelligence of strategic thinking. We need leaders whose stories can inform us as well as guide us. We need leaders who touch our hearts and awaken our minds. We need leaders who have found their inspiration. These leaders understand the ultimate divine breath of life—to live in the ebb and flow of a force that is greater than one's self; to connect to a purpose that is higher than one's self. This sort of inspiration, coupled with openness and transparency, is the root of inspirational presence.

LEADERS WITH INSPIRATIONAL PRESENCE

Our world needs leaders with inspirational presence, who are connected to a greater truth for their own direction. These leaders, when engaged, are transparent, authentic, and present, and they lead from a place that is outside of their ordinary self. They exhibit a style that is uniquely different, that is noticeable from a distance.

One of the questions I'm asked most frequently is "What do I have to do to be inspirational?" The answer to this is so simple that it sounds flippant: "Be inspired." This is the first place of leadership. Each of us has to find the thing in life that really turns us on, that lights up our eyes, that makes us want to leap out of bed in the morning because we can't wait to be involved with it. We find our passion in the middle of this space of caring, and we learn that our actions produce results, and create things that we can love. At a basic level, we learn to operate from a place of love that is in action. When we see people who have this energy flowing through them, we will see it in their eyes. We will hear it in their voices. We will feel it through their actions.

We have a choice as leaders, whether we will spend our time trying to get other people to do things and see things in a certain way, or to generally accomplish goals that are of our own making. When we look at leaders who have found their inspiration and have connected in that deep way of being and knowing, we see that they are on a journey and are setting their own pace. These people truly lead by creating the spiritual, emotional, and cognitive journey toward their highest aspirations. They do not propel others in that direction. They compel others to want the same things. That is the deep and profound difference of this leadership style.

The people around this type of leader pick up this energy and literally begin to feel the inspiration as well. They start to respond and move their energy in a like direction and look to their "emotional leader" as a bellwether for what is important on the horizon and how to respond to situations in the here and now.

LEADERSHIP AND THE LIMBIC SYSTEM

Here is where we begin to understand the biomechanical aspect of inspirational presence. Our limbic system is a system of organs, nerves, glands, and portions of our brain that function together to govern our emotions. The significant feature for leadership is that it is an *open-loop* system—that means that it can take input from outside of the system. In a social group, the interaction of a group of people's limbic systems is referred to as social contagion (from the same root as the word *contagious*), one of the most pronounced and obvious being laughter. If we go to a comedy club and sit in a room full of people who are laughing, the show likely will seem uproariously funny. If we were to watch the same routine on television, however, we probably would not have the same response because we would be missing the group experience of shared emotion.

This example shows how people experience contagion that is spread across a crowd. There are many different ways that contagion can be played out, although some of the most widely known are somewhat negative— mass hysteria, riots, and other greatly heightened group emotional reactions. The positive effect is felt in group meditations, peace marches, or other times when people share a collective intention and expand on a shared positive emotion. When we move into the same physical space and share emotional experiences, we see the effects of contagion.

We know that we humans connect through the open loops of our limbic systems, as we send and receive energy to everyone and everything around us. It is easy to know, from an intuitive sense, that we actually experience other people's energy and their emotional states, and we can find ourselves influenced by others around us. Most people can relate to having been with another person whose energy and emotional state was so uplifting that they began to feel uplifted as well. Similarly, most people can relate to spending time around a person who is depressed, soon finding their own energy dwindling to match the other person's energy.

This sort of empathic response has a deep physiological origin. To truly understand what is happening, it is helpful to remember that modern people have evolved from primeval packs and tribes. The original social unit was quite small, and early humans lived together to survive. Our earliest survival instincts are embedded deeply within a social structure. This survives in today's family unit, where we have a basic system of interdependency into which most of us are born. This structure is literally part of our physiology, as our nervous system has developed in such a way as to take advantage of others around us for protection, companionship, and security.

Our brains have evolved in such a way as to rapidly process this information and act upon it. The oldest portion of the brain is at the juncture of the spinal cord and the brain and is called the amygdule. It is also referred to as the "reptilian brain" or the primitive brain. This portion of the brain developed millennia before the frontal lobes and the higher order processing that is handled there. The amygdule has some very basic functions. It looks at information in front of us and processes it through survival functions. Is it something we need to kill, eat, mate with, or ignore? This is the location for "fight, flight, freeze, or follow." These primordial functions are what kept humans alive and the species perpetuated.

Through the years, the frontal lobes developed to a point of taking over most of the higher-order processing and dealing with the world in a more rules-based and rational fashion. This, however, has not taken the amygdule out of the equation. It is still alive and well and wired into our hormonal system to provide us with all the energy we need to chase down a mastodon or flee a saber-toothed tiger. Its evolutionary path has been slow and has maintained its old focus through the millennia.

Our emotions are associated with hormonal states in our bodies. There seems to be a correlation effect, not necessarily a cause-and-effect relationship. In other words, emotions and hormone levels tend to be predictably associated. One can expect that with certain hormonal changes, predictable emotions will follow. For instance, if an athlete begins taking steroids and bringing up his testosterone levels, it is fairly predictable that emotional outbursts ('roid rages) will follow.

Another example of this is related to fear. If we watch a particularly scary movie, we begin to feel the fear in our bodies. If it is strong enough, we will even begin to taste the adrenaline response. Our hearts will race; our breathing will quicken. To take that even farther, days later, just thinking about that movie may produce the same effect. The brain does not really know the difference between something fearful being in front of it or our just thinking about something frightening. Let's expand this even more. After we've watched the really scary movie, it is possible that that night will be filled with noises and unidentified shapes that can quickly be identified as terrible threats (usually imagined). The point here is that our hormonal systems and our brains are joined in ways that work together to create our reality. If we get scared, our brains will quickly begin finding more threats. At the same time, if we get calm and trusting, our brains will quickly begin finding opportunities and possibilities. A fearful mind looks for bad things, and a calm mind looks for good things.

Going back to the correlation effect, if we start thinking about threats, our bodies will correspondingly create the hormonal reactions that are associated with fight-or-flight. If we start thinking about creative opportunities, we get an altogether different hormonal response. Our stress levels go down, we relax more, and our thinking becomes more expansive.

Furthermore, we also know that consistently living in specific emotional states, such as anger, also are followed by a physiological change. Ultimately, we will change at a biological, or cellular, level to be consistent with an overall recurring emotional state. For example, when a cell that has been loaded with the peptide response to anger divides, it creates a new cell that "wants" that same level of anger peptides. At that point, the biological need will trigger the brain to look for reasons to be angry in order to satisfy the cellular need for the hormonal response to anger. By the same token, if we have developed a body that lives in heightened states of happiness, our cells will call out for events that will fill the cellular need for happiness. Either one can impact the other, or they work both ways. Our bodies can become habitually tied to a hormonal and emotional state, and therefore, it becomes the energy that we project to others, just by getting close to them.

What does this have to do with leadership, and why are we talking about it now? The answer goes back to the social evolution of a tribe. While we are talking about the individual phenomenon of the emotional/mental/physical connection, there is also a group connection of the same sort. This is another function of the limbic system.

To fully make the connection to leadership, we need to remember the social aspect of tribal living, with deep similarities to how pack animals operate. We are born with our limbic systems attuned to our mothers. That continues in life, as we learn to attune to others to provide information in social settings. We learn to follow the lead in our family systems of people to whom we give authority to keep us safe or to give us guidance. That continues throughout our lives and shows up in every group setting we experience.

As we move through groups during the course of life, each one of us is transmitting emotional information to others around us as well as receiving emotional information from those same people. As we spend more time together, as when we establish a team or social group, the limbic systems of that group will learn an order of emotional listening and develop a pattern of emotions that plays out predictably when that group comes together. The key for leaders is that every group, at a deep and subconscious level, is looking for the person in that group who is the emotional leader and who will provide group direction and guidance. If there is a social hierarchy at play, those patterns help the group attune to a person more quickly and consistently. For instance, if the group knows that a particular person is "in charge", the individuals tend to look first to that person for leadership signals before they look elsewhere. In the absence of clear leadership signals, the group will move to any strong emotion that feels compelling—but this can be very destructive.

We can see many examples of groups where the emotional leadership arises from a basis of fear. British psychoanalyst W. R. Bion said that the natural leader of a group would be the one who was the most paranoid and the first to find a reason to enter an emotional state of fight-or-flight.

In context, Bion was working with British soldiers during World War II who had just been evacuated from Dunkirk and were suffering from "shell shock," as it was called at the time. (We would now term this post-traumatic stress disorder, or PTSD.) These men had every reason to feel traumatized and paranoid at that time, but the significance here still remains clear. Leadership of a group can come from a place of fear, distrust, and doubt. The limbic system works either way, and a group follows either way. As we talk about leadership, it becomes increasingly clear that the emotional state of a leader is absolutely critical. Also, every group will eventually find a source of leadership. Whoever is the formal leader of a group either can lead it—or watch it be led.

Daniel Goleman's work *Emotional Intelligence* (1996) points out some other more positive examples of why the emotional state of the leader is important. It is clear from the research on emotions and leadership in the workplace that positive moods have a positive correlation to productivity and job performance. By the same token, moods like anger, resentment, and hostility can have a negative impact on job performance and increase turnover in the workplace. I believe that we all know this correlation from our experience in life. How many of us have found ourselves making errors at critical times, simply because we are in a bad mood? Or, when we have felt great, we've noticed that all of our tasks seem to be easier and faster. Many of the leaders with whom I have worked have described this correlation as intuitively obvious, to the point of labeling it with the Disney tune of "Whistle While You Work." Indeed, intuition is a strong part of our ability as humans to lead others, to navigate social networks, and to create a path through uncharted regions. Most of us know this from experience. If we are in a relationship of any sort—work, family, romantic, or social—where the mood is unhappy, heavy, or depressing, we feel ourselves dragged down. We will feel uninspired. Conversely, if that same situation has optimism and enthusiasm, we will feel that mood moving through us as well. How often, in even the smallest ways, has a social setting inspired us to try something? People who are in emotionally safe, trusting, and supportive environments take more risks. They feel freer to be creative and spontaneous.

Try this out for yourself—based on your experience, can you feel the difference in your own performance based on mood? The Dali Lama states it this way: "Choose optimism. It feels better."

Here, I am making a point for leadership. While there are many, many research studies that basically illustrate the correlational impact of emotions and job performance, discussing those in depth would talk to your head. In order to fully grasp the leadership concept discussed in this book, I ask you to take a different approach. The type of leader described here is balanced in approaching the world through his or her head, heart, and gut. At this point, if you can access the body and emotional memory you have of the impact of emotions on your productivity and levels of inspiration, you will begin to live from this model. That which you become aware of in yourself and consciously access will begin to shape your life. When you feel this, you begin to develop the empathy that helps you understand what a group of people needs at any given time. From there, you begin the journey of learning to lead through your presence.

LEADERSHIP AND AUTHORITY

It's time to make another clear distinction—what we are *not* talking about here. Very often the word "leader" is used euphemistically to mean "boss" or other authority figure. In those cases, it is used to indicate who is in charge through his or her formal authority and also to elevate the importance of what that person is doing. In reality, a large percentage of people who have the title or designation of *leader* are not leading at all. They may be directing or providing managerial functions, but they are not leading. They are in positions to exercise power through authority.

Renowned sociologist Max Weber outlined three different types of authority in his "tripartite classification." He described charismatic authority, traditional authority, and rational formal authority. Each of these is a description of how authority is established within a group of people in order to achieve consistent social behavior. All of these are useful in understanding how power is used in society and how various social behaviors can occur or not occur. He describes the charismatic authority of historical figures, such as Jesus and Mohammed, and how their deep personal beliefs and powerful presence achieved authority over society to such an extent as to have people change their beliefs and social practices to follow their way. He noted the social phenomenon of "routinization of charisma," which occurs when others take the personal authority granted to a person and create a formal and rational authority base to replicate it. An example is the charismatic authority Jesus possessed that was later adopted into organized religions that claimed a heritage of authority based on following his teachings. In this manner, the charismatic authority was transferred into the formal authority of religion.

Yet this only describes authority and not leadership. While Jesus might have had the personal power to tell people what to say or do, it is doubtful that he would have been so direct or so controlling. It is more likely that he honored choice in every way. By the same token, when we look at the writings of the Buddha, we get the same sense of engagement with others. While he might have shown people how they could achieve enlightenment, he was not out to direct their behavior or to control what they did or did not do. Instead, both of these people presented a series of personal choices. As they stood in the place of enlightenment, they beckoned others to join them.

This distinction of authority is one of control and power. This is crucial to understanding true leadership. When we talk about leadership, we lean toward having people who follow because they want to, not because they have to. When we get into the social nuances of empowered systems, we see that this type of leadership is generous and allows others to share in the direction and to expand on their own passions as well. This allows for the synergy of groups and allows the natural phenomenon of collective consciousness to do the creative designs on its own.

In this book, leadership is described as an act and a practice. A person who is in a position of authority and who has extended impact over the lives of others must also lead. Calling a person a leader does not make him or her one. Giving a person a supervisory, managerial, or executive position does not make him or her a leader. It simply gives that person authority. This distinction is called personal and positional power. People in authority roles have positional power, but they also need to develop their personal power. Many times, this will seem paradoxical, as such people will wonder why they need to develop the ability to cause other people to take action because they want to—rather, these people may feel they have the authority to *make* other people take action, even if they don't want to. In truth, a sustainable organization is built through a shared intention of a group of people, not the control actions of one. This comes through the peoples' collective choice to follow the passion of its leadership, whether one person or many.

As you develop your personal ability to lead, remember that all groups want leadership at a primordial level and will find it without any external stimulus. The most compelling and constructive leadership for groups comes through calm, assertive, and deeply inspired direction. One does not need to use power to lead a group but will use whatever power is available toward an external mission. When you lead from a place of inspiration, people will naturally gravitate toward you. Your ability to sustain that passion and maintain your direction will keep them with you.

In summary, we have examined several aspects of leadership and why the ability to inspire others matters. Our ideal of a connected and dynamic leadership starts from a place of solid personal inspiration. It is about the power of purpose—of passion—and it leads to an engaging style of personal connection. This leadership runs deeply through the limbic system and creates a web of emotional connection through the phenomenon of contagion. Leaders who come from a place of inspirational presence have an effect on groups that stimulates their creativity, opens their sense of vision, and expands their thinking. These leaders offer a compelling direction for others and lead through their passion and heart connections, rather than through power, control, or authority. While there are compelling reasons from a human perspective to lead from this stance, there is also strong evidence of the positive impact it can have on organizational performance. Let us take some first steps in learning how to embody this leadership style.

QUESTIONS TO ASK YOURSELF

Inspiration
- When have I felt the most inspired?
- What was I doing, thinking about, learning, or living?
- Am I still doing that?
- Can I get more of that in my life?

Presence
- Whom have I known whose presence I felt from a distance?
- What was it about that person that got my attention?
- What do I know about how that person lived that made him or her unique?
- How transparent am I?
- How do others experience me?

Power
- How important is the use of power to me?
- Do I know when I most want to use power to get my way?
- Whom have I seen use power in the most advanced and constructive way?

Authority
- What is my tendency to lean on authority in my relationships with others?
- How does authority impact me? Do I rely on a person's authority to inform me how to relate to them?
- What is the most positive and constructive way I know to use authority?

Exercise for advancement

Take some time to write out a description of how you will be when you are leading from a place of inspiration, and you have opened yourself to others in an authentic way. Pick the time frame in the future. Include all of your senses. Write down how others will perceive you and what this ability will allow for you in your life.

CHAPTER 2—LEARNING TO LEAD

*You can't teach what you don't know, and
you can't lead where you won't go.*

—Rev. Jesse Jackson

Although we talk about leadership as if it is a new science, it is a topic that has been explored for millennia. Many different approaches to leadership have been well documented and studied. When you begin a deeper study of the subject, you will find that there are numerous starting points. Some are based on the ability to manipulate others (à la Niccolò Machiavelli) or to lead armies to victory (à la Sun Tzu); some focus on skills and behaviors (à la Kurt Lewin); some look at the motivational ability of the leader (à la David McClelland); some are based in power (à la John Kotter); and some are based in authority (à la Max Weber). Each of these has its success story and obviously makes sense in some context. This approach to leadership is a combination of two groups of skills: individual and group. The group skills are essential to overall leadership ability, but the basis is in the individual, with who you are as a person and where you want to go.

The act of leadership is a combination of skills and unique worldviews that combine to allow leaders the flexibility to create new conditions, to move the hearts and minds of others, and to manifest reality that would not have emerged otherwise. There have been many individuals who have exhibited great leadership in their fields, including (among others) artists, scientists, scholars, musicians, and explorers. Their pioneering efforts created new possibilities and encouraged change around them from people who had learned from either their example or their tutelage. Many of these pioneers had little or no interest in whether anyone else went in the same direction as they went. They were simply following their own passion. That, in itself, is a fundamental part of leadership—the piece that begins at home, deep in the soul of the creator. That is the part that cannot be falsified. It is true passion. Very often, these people lead by creating movements or new thoughts that others imitate or adopt later. The act of individual creativity, however, often does not have a number of immediate followers, nor does it necessarily have the intention of having others follow.

Then there is another category of leaders, those who are emphatic in their desire for others to share in their path and to create better conditions for many people. These leaders are much more concerned about the efforts and results of groups of people, not just their own efforts. The ability to lead yourself and follow your own passion is still the starting point, but this form of leadership also requires a broader understanding of how groups and organizations work. These leaders must have a means to fully grasp and order the entire system with which they are working. For example, a person with a passion for clean fuels and a sustainable environment can spend his time in the lab creating the technologies, or he can become a social activist, creating broad change that requires clean fuels and a sustainable environment. Each would have different levels of involvement at the group level. While the first example requires the creative spirit and discipline of personal passion, much of that energy is turned toward the technology and mechanics. In the second, much of the energy is turned toward the people who are using that technology. Both require the fundamental passion to fuel the creativity. Both are immensely valuable to our world, and both have their lessons. Both can benefit from the ability to tap into their inspiration and allow their presence to impact the people with whom they are dealing.

LEADERSHIP STARTS AT HOME— WHO ARE YOU AND WHERE ARE YOU GOING?

I have heard two approaches to living your life. One old adage is "Bloom where you are planted." I greatly admire and respect the ability of people who make the most of any situation. Martin Luther King, Jr., said it like this: "If it falls your lot to be a street sweeper, sweep streets as Rafael painted pictures, sweep streets as Michelangelo carved marble, sweep streets as Beethoven composed music or as Shakespeare wrote poetry." This approach is a fundamental part of being present and fully putting your love, light, and humanity into whatever situation you encounter. There is a real beauty in this approach to life.

The second approach is to go out and create your own life. This involves an inward journey to begin finding more than just where you have wound up on this planet. This means finding where you want to be. From here, you can actively step out and find a pathway to a destination that only you have imagined.

Ideally, a leadership journey would involve a combination of the two. You would decide the destination and path, then fully engage every moment along the way with full passion and commitment to experience the joy of the journey.

In the last chapter, I spoke of leaders who found their inspiration and, through that, inspired others to places of greatness. This is one point of paradox in this model. Those people who are most connected with their source of power and inspiration are often the least concerned with directing or controlling what others do. They are, in their deepest and most sincere places, driven to direct their own actions. This deep and innate personal commitment is what creates the sense of tribal unity that causes others to work their hardest to move in the same direction as their leader.

These leaders usually want particular outcomes in the world, and they want for other people to share in particular sensibilities. In a business setting, the global leader definitely wants for people in the organization to pay attention to particular areas and details but usually only to the degree that these areas produce certain results. This leader will hope that the people in the organization actually want the same things and that their desires guide constructive action.

There is a very simple path to accomplishing this basic and essential first step of leadership. Here's the formula:

1. Find your passion—that is the thing that you most love and want to have happen in the world.
2. Connect with your passion on a deep and personal level. Become an expert. Make it an integral part of the fabric of your life and the essence of your being.

3. Launch your passion into the world in a big, big way. Imagine the greatest possible contribution that you can make; double that, then double it again, then figure out how you can live it into being every day of your life.

Simple, right? Well, actually, it is. We begin early in life with this, learning things that interest us, excelling in sports, learning music, becoming artists, engineers, architects, and engaging in other creative pursuits. We initiate this process in small ways, but as we become more conscious and aware, our interests start to shift to larger and more socially connected issues. As we grow beyond the point of being able to do it all ourselves, we enter the realm of influence, where we must begin to rely on others for our dreams to be fully realized. We expand our passions from areas of interest to hobbies to life purposes. Along the way, those areas of interest will probably change. What will remain constant is the skill that you have acquired in learning to engage an idea and hold it in a deeply important place.

While it may seem formulaic and perhaps daunting, it is an absolute requirement. If you cannot be inspired, how can you ever hope to inspire others? If you cannot find your own way, why would anyone ever choose to follow you?

Each of us comes to this life with something to accomplish. We have our core lessons to learn, and our core contribution to make. Every aspect of our lives weaves together to form a tapestry that is unique in every sense, with its own beauty and sense of purpose. Humans are creative and generative beings. During the time we walk this planet, some of us will find that place and will live life to its fullest, contributing to the society and the evolution of humanity. Others will not, regardless of the opportunities or the deep desires they may have.

This first step of leadership is of great importance. It is not necessarily about finding the one thing that is our deepest and truest purpose for all of time, although we may aspire to do that. More often it tends to be learning to search, find, move, and learn. Many people's purpose shifts throughout life, as we try out different ways of being and as we experiment with different paths. Mine certainly has. At times, my sense of mission seemed to turn sharply. Other times, it just seemed to course correct.

The trend has been mostly one of sharpening, with the mission gradually becoming clearer. It has also become far simpler than in the early stages. More recently, I have found how all of the seemingly disparate parts that I lived earlier in life integrate into a more robust ability to deliver on a very simple mission.

It is perfectly acceptable to refine a sense of mission. Ideally, the process of refining will have us actually move through the redefined mission, not away from it. From there, we will adjust to our next sense of mission. Often we will transition into an endeavor, and while there, discover some aspect that is even more important or deeply satisfying. If that is the case, then move with it. That is ultimately being true to ourselves. If we give up on a mission because it seems too big or scary, then we are just giving up on ourselves.

To find true passion, we simply have to look inside at what really matters. Just tapping into our awareness can usually create enough guidance to tell us what is important and what is not. As we will discuss later, we must evaluate and question our mission through reflection on the actions we take. We will know if a mission feels right only when we try to live it.

MANAGING YOURSELF

In order to lead others, you must first lead yourself. More than anything else, this should become a practice throughout your life. A nice way to look at this is through the idea that you already have a leadership practice. We all do. The question is whether or not you know it and whether you put conscious energy toward how you engage that practice.

I use the word practice here to connote something that you regularly do and how you approach the world. Every thought and every action constitutes the whole of how you are defined as a leader. Deeply imbedded in this practice are the words you use, your self-talk, and your habitual responses to the world. The basic difference between a habit and a practice is mindfulness. Once you become mindful of how you talk to yourself, you can understand that those words and emotions are a rehearsal for how you will talk to others. Once you become mindful of the habitual stories you tell yourself about the world (your personal mythology), you become mindful of how those stories become a guide for your interactions and the explanations you place on the world.

You can lead by claiming the inherent power of these natural dynamics and using them for positive purpose. It simply requires noticing what is going through your mind and deciding whether that is the most appropriate view of the world at the time. You decide whether your behaviors match the current situation. You determine the energy that you want to put into the world. In every given moment, you have the option of seeing the world through a loving and trusting lens or through one of fear and doubt. In every action you take, you have the choice of creating positive and creative situations or negative and destructive ones.

In order to frame this, there are certain areas where you can focus your attention to begin this practice. Each has a particular purpose in creating a solid and dynamic leader, and each affords a particular area of personal power. We will take these separately.

THE POWER OF INTENTION

Intention is defined as "an anticipated outcome that guides your planned actions." This breaks down into two distinct parts. First, understanding your "anticipated outcome" and second, "guiding your planned actions." Many people don't realize how much this plays out on a daily basis. For instance, how often have you seen a person (maybe yourself) walk into a situation expecting a negative outcome? For instance, let's consider Sara, who holds a belief that meetings are a waste of time and nothing good ever happens there. She enters a staff meeting just knowing that it will be terrible (anticipated outcome) and, consequently, she sits idly and waits for it to go south (guides planned action). However, if you were to say to Sara that her intention was to have a bad meeting, she would probably disagree with you.

This is referred to as the *Law of Attraction*, which states that whatever we think about, believe, and focus our energy on is what we create for our lives—and it is important in our daily practice of life to know how to use this law. What Sara would probably say is that she just knew it would happen that way. She might even say that she really wanted to have a good meeting but felt it was beyond her control, and she might cite that as evidence that meetings are indeed a waste of time. At this level, what she is expressing is more like a wish. We get to be a leader when we add the power of our own dynamic presence, when we see the highest possible anticipated outcome and use ourselves in the moment to create that outcome. This is when we transform a passive wish into a clear intention.

It is really a question of consciousness and choice. As a leader, it is a requirement that we get very clear about the anticipated outcomes that we are carrying around. Intention ties in quite closely with our conscious and subconscious belief systems. As such, we can be carrying a negative limiting belief at a subconscious level that operates as a default guide—not a good thing for being a dynamic and powerful leader. For the purpose of leadership practice, we need to get clear on what we see as anticipated outcomes and use them to guide our actions in a way that helps us accomplish positive things.

Let's use one example of conversations: At a very discreet level, we can think of each conversation we have as an opportunity to connect with our deepest beliefs and frame them into an intention. When you sit down to talk to someone, think about what it is that you want to accomplish through this time. Think about what is important to you and to the other person. After that, be clear about why you are having this conversation. Express what you say as an intention, as in "It is my intention to connect at an emotional level" or "It is my intention to get clear on our weekly priorities." You can do this silently or, more powerfully, to the participants. From there, let that intention guide your actions.

Now, be careful—there is a potential downside to this. If you only focus on what you want to accomplish, you probably won't get it. Communicating is building a system of rapport between people, and that requires healthy amounts of paying attention to the other person's wants and needs. If we turn our intention into an agenda, we run the risk of shutting out other people.

Make it a practice to consistently be as clear as possible about your intentions for all of the things you do on a daily basis. Think about your intention in writing an email. Think about your intention in reading an email. Think about your intention when you greet a receptionist or the server in a restaurant. Think about your intention when you say hello to significant people in your life. Whatever it is, the greater degree to which we can bring up our "anticipated outcomes" and make them consciously our own, the more effective, dynamic, and powerful we will be in the world.

THE POWER OF COMMITMENT

Ultimately, the power you will have as a leader of yourself and your own personal journey comes down to how much and what kind of energy you direct toward your passion and mission in life. Recognizing and honoring commitment allows you to choose your actions. Here's an interesting way to look at this: You will hear about people being committed or not committed when you look at what they are doing or not doing. These words are typically uttered to describe a person who is not doing something that someone feels that person should be doing.

But what if you saw everyone as completely committed to the choices they made? A person can be committed to indifference or committed to ambiguity. A person who is having trouble deciding what he wants to do can be committed to indecision or committed to struggling. What if every action people took was because they were committed to that path? Consider how that would change your view of them.

At that level, it brings a completely new wrinkle to how you work with yourself and with others. It means that you do not have to make yourself commit; just recognize where you are already committed and decide whether that is what you truly want. At the deepest level, your power comes when you recognize that everyone is profoundly committed to creating the life he or she is leading, exactly the way it is. If you are not getting what you think you want, you must find the areas of commitment that you want to shift. Until you become aware of them, they remain invisible forces that can keep you from moving in desired areas.

You commence the alignment of your intentions with your being through commitment. It shows up in every area of your life and can be used both to change your behaviors and to clarify your intention. Let's go back to our example of Sara and her attitude toward meetings. We can say that Sara is committed to having bad meetings and committed to her opinion of the value of meetings through her recurring actions. If she examines her intentions and claims that she truly wants good meetings, then it is up to her to commit to her intention through personal leadership. First, she has to commit to mental images of what happens in good meetings. She has to commit to using language, both with others and in her self-talk, that is consistent with that intention. Finally, when she is in the meetings, she has to commit her energy, thoughts, and efforts to the meeting process. It is only through actively recognizing her previous commitment to bad meetings that she can shift her own power to an aligned commitment and begin releasing her personal power.

At the most basic level, you can begin by acknowledging that you are absolutely committed to everything in your life, exactly as it is right now. The question is, do you want to be? If you are not getting what you want in life and are, instead, getting things you don't want, you must look at how your are committing yourself—through your energy, thoughts, words, and actions—to creating your life precisely as it is. Some people find this daunting or even overwhelming, but the great positive is that if you believe this, it absolutely follows that you can create something else, simply by committing to that new set of ideals and releasing the conflicting commitments.

THE POWER OF SAYING YES

We need to send very clear messages to ourselves and to the universe surrounding us as to what we really want and deserve. It is a clear and simple act to say yes to these things in life. This means getting very clear about what yes truly means. While we may have the moment in life where we received the outcome we most desired and we say a resounding yes, there is also the moment in life when we get something that we truly do not want. We simply accept it as part of the world. That, too, is saying yes to a condition. Remember, our subconscious really cannot tell the difference. Whatever we say yes to in life, we get more of it. Living in an abusive relationship is saying yes to that pattern in your life. Living with a job that you do not like enough is saying yes to those conditions and emotions.

Part of the art of leadership is beginning to understand the things to which you are saying yes and how you are saying it. Obviously, we first need to clarify those things that we most want and desire; we need to begin to find examples of where they exist in our world and clearly and firmly affirm them in powerful yes messages.

THE POWER OF SAYING NO

Often, when people begin describing their intentions, they talk a lot about what they *don't* want and how they are going to get rid of it. That is very important and is, in fact, a prerequisite to be able to attain anything. As we know from studying the systems theory of the interaction of any organism in its environment, there are always things that the organism wants (goals) and things that the organism wants to avoid (noxiants). People are the same way. We want to get as much of the good stuff in life as we can while avoiding as much of the bad stuff (however we each define those).

Nonetheless, it is not very powerful to write a goal statement from a place of avoidance, as in "I don't want to overreact," or "I don't want to overeat," or "I don't want to lose money in the stock market," or "I don't want to scare my employees." This actually focuses your attention on the negative condition and increases the likelihood that you will get more of it. We talk about this, in simple terms, as writing a goal in *toward* language rather than *away from*.

At a deeper level, though, we humans have a continuous energetic exchange with the universe, in which we are constantly training our subconscious as to what we really want in life. The Law of Attraction does not understand away from, only toward. As with all laws, there is no judgment or evaluation attached to the objects of our attention. In fact, the entire concept of goals and noxiants is a human concept, outside of what exists in nature. The Law of Attraction is much simpler than that. Anything that occupies our mental energy is expanded and brought into our life in greater quantities.

With that, it becomes vitally important that we learn to say no to the things that do not fit our particular vision of how we want to exist in this life. A good friend of mine once said, "Until I hear and understand your no, your yes means nothing." Take that to an energetic level and begin to understand that you are constantly telling your subconscious where to focus energy. By saying no to the things in life that do not fit your path, you allow extra mindshare to dedicate to your heartfelt yes.

By saying no to what does not fit, you do yourself—and everyone else—a great service. If something in your life does not work, begin saying no to it. At the same time, find those parts of your life that most fit your highest purpose and align with your path, and practice actively saying yes to those things. The power of no is in defining boundaries. This, in turn, provides clarity and power to every yes that follows.

THE POWER OF SAYING AND

Prioritize. Make tough choices. Be selective. These are some things that leaders often are called upon to do. This approach, however, can create a tendency at times for leaders to get locked into a pattern of exclusion. When most people think of priorities, they think of this or that. They think about which choice they will make, and as a result, what will go undone. Prioritization is often associated with making sacrifices and only being able to do some of the really good things we would like to do.

While this is a great practice and requires the skill of discernment, it can become, like anything else, an overused approach to leadership. Real leadership always considers how thoughts engage other people and how we create a consciousness for success among groups of people.

The other way to think of these things is in an "and" world. How do I create more market share *and* drive down costs? This is at one level, but I think that all of us need to consider some far more important *and* questions.

I once worked with the CEO of an environmental science group. He made this statement: "We would like to be able to make all the power we want *and* have healthy fish populations." That really stuck with me. I think about that often. How do we have plenty of energy *and* a clean planet for future generations? How do we create solid, healthy communities *and* create global awareness? How do we create lives that enjoy the abundance of this earth *and* preserve it for future generations?

Each of us, in all of our individual endeavors, needs to consider the important *ands* of our businesses. As our global connectivity increases, there is no more hiding in one corner of the world. We are an interconnected globe, and we all need to learn to act as such. The ability to understand, identify, and relate to multiple stakeholder groups and maintain these multiple perspectives is one of the most important ands we can have for our world.

THE POWER OF EMPATHY

Empathy is the basic capacity of humans to relate to others through the emotional information we sense by tuning into others' experiences. The absence of empathy creates the psychopath. Empathy guides us and allows us to join into groups with some feeling of safety or to steer away from situations that seem unsafe. It provides us with the opportunity for deep personal connections. It creates emotional bonds in groups. Expanded empathy leads to heightened intuition. Empathy is an absolute requirement for effective leadership.

Empathy is a complex set of behaviors and processes that we learn over time. To understand it, we must realize that it comes into play through an interaction between the frontal lobes of our brain and our amygdula, the most primitive part of our brain, where our fight-or-flight responses live. When we are born, our amygdula is nearly fully developed, whereas it takes our frontal lobes until we are in our twenties to develop fully. During that time, we learn about what our experiences mean and determine the useful information for us in life. Through these interactions, we create a set of beliefs that forms the basis for internal conversations between the frontal lobes and the amygdula about what actually occurs around us.

Our amygdula is the first part of our brain to perceive information from our feelings about others. We look at another person, and our feelings respond first. The amygdula is the fastest processor in the brain, although it takes in less information than other areas. It is high speed and low resolution. The amygdula processes simultaneously with the frontal lobe, which is low speed and high resolution. Because of the dynamic between the two parts of our brain, most events that we encounter that have an emotional content are first interpreted by our amygdula and then by our frontal lobe.

Our first and potentially strongest emotional response is sometimes one that we learned earliest in life, maybe as young as age four or five. When we begin thinking about our thinking and thinking about our feelings, we begin to teach our amygdula new responses, and that allows us to move into a stronger and more mature state of connection with others. When we were four or five years old, our responses were dependent in nature. With maturity, we learn to be independent, then interdependent. Through mindfulness, we learn how to feel what is happening with others and have it guide mature and connected action on our part. This is how we begin to lead in confusing or chaotic environments.

We learn to train our minds to take on our belief sets and expand our ability to connect with others in meaningful and powerful ways. Through this, we can consciously choose how we engage with other people and how we use the power of empathy to relate to others. As a leader, this skill is fundamental to leading and influencing others. We first understand where others are by stepping into their experience and understanding how it would be for us.

THE POWER OF INTEGRATION

As we begin to take responsibility for our lives and the impact we have on the world, we must grow increasingly clear about how we spend our time and energy. We have discussed how we created our life exactly as it is and how we must begin to choose the areas that will occupy our consciousness. As we begin to work with larger groups of people and our passions take us to areas of increased complexity, we are presented with the opportunity to get feedback about our own focuses and blind spots, as well as to encounter people who have significantly different focuses.

Personal growth is often defined as the ability to reach out and claim parts of ourselves that have been previously ignored—or worse, hated and ignored. We often undervalue or even disavow personal traits simply because they remind us of someone, something, or sometime that is unpleasant to us. It can be because we never felt confident in a particular area, or we were so focused in one area that we thought the other was a waste of time and energy.

Similar to the way in which we learn to do with ourselves, as leaders we often omit parts of constituent groups because of our own personal limits to perception or even our own biases. We must be able to transcend feelings of competitiveness or exclusion and work from a place of inclusion, where we can integrate a large variety of seemingly different groups of people and help them achieve mutual success. You develop this ability by first learning how to integrate all parts of yourself.

MICROTRANSFORMATIONS

Transformations indicate that there is a fundamental change in perception, in state, or in basic usability of an object or practice. We often talk about transformation in social systems, as when the rules of operation change. This can be experienced by moving to another country and immersing yourself in a different culture and lifestyle. We can also experience it by moving from one corporation to another, when suddenly we no longer know how to function. Culture can be seen as "how we do things around here," which translates into making schemas for groups of people.

When you begin taking on your own lifestyle and engagement process with the world, you begin to learn how to create transformations.

For the most part, these are seemingly small and, at times, barely noticeable. However, each time you chose your language to be in alignment with your mission, you create microtransformations. This is the essence of transformation leadership—learning how to take the smallest situation and transform it into a more positive, aligned, and affirming experience for yourself.

In *The Four Agreements* (1997), Don Miguel Ruez lists the first agreement you make with yourself as this: "Be impeccable with your word." I find this to be brilliant, conscious, and, at times, really challenging. In leadership, this extends far beyond an obvious connotation of doing what you say you are going to do. It is about choosing your words with deep intention and clarity. Understand the power your words have. Look at the language you use with yourself, and be impeccable in how you speak to yourself at all times and in all situations. This will immediately begin transforming your experience of the world.

Once you begin noticing these microtransformations in yourself, you can begin to notice how your language and intentions impact others. The largest changes in the world are made up of multitudes of microtransformations across many people.

QUESTIONS TO ASK YOURSELF

Intention
- What intentions do I have in life?
- Do I carry intentions that have not served me? What are they?

Commitment
- To what am I deeply committed in line with my mission?
- How do I show it?
- To what am I deeply committed that is out of line with my mission and perhaps keeps me from moving in a direction I would like to go?
- How do I show it?

Yes
- To what things have I said yes in life?
- How do I show that?
- Am I being true to that yes?
- Are there things to which I need to say an emphatic yes?
- What's stopping me?

No
- To what things have I said no in life?
- How do I show that?
- Am I being true to that no?
- Are there things to which I need to say an emphatic no?
- What's stopping me?

And
- How do I view prioritization?
- How exclusionary am I in my language around priorities?
- Do I see the practice of prioritization as being about sacrifice?

Empathy
- How do I connect with what experiences are like for others?
- Do I get interested in what is important to others?
- Do I look at leadership as the ability to get what is important for me or as the ability to help others get what is important for them?

Integration
- What parts of myself do I feel I have left behind?
- What parts of myself am I trying to suppress?
- How can I learn to take the positive aspects of these parts into my life and mission today?

Exercise for advancement
- What are the most important things I am trying to create today in my life and in business?
- What important things do I feel that I have to give up to accomplish these things (my time, my health, my family, my money, etc.)?
- Create a statement that puts them both together (e.g., I want to deliver and maintain/expand).
- Given my current mission or objective in life, what are the gifts of each of these to its accomplishment?
- How will I expand my awareness and action to integrate the other perspectives and positions?

CHAPTER 3—
COMMITMENT TO CHOICE

We who lived in concentration camps can remember the men who walked through the huts comforting others, giving away their last piece of bread. They may have been few in number, but they offer sufficient proof that everything can be taken from a man but one thing: the last of the human freedoms—to choose one's attitude in any given set of circumstances, to choose one's own way.

—Viktor Frankl

To approach life through inspirational leadership requires a radical departure from a need to control. Many organizational policies will label executives as leaders, possibly just to acknowledge an organizational expectation, possibly to attempt to posture these executives in a more powerful light with the organization, or perhaps simply to wish this to be true. Real leaders in life know that they actually have very little control over the people in their organizations and even less regarding what goes on around and outside of their organization. While they may be rightfully concerned with the stability and control of the situation, it is not about being controlling. It is about having an organization that is designed to provide its own control, without trying to control the people within it. The key to this approach is in recognizing and honoring choice in their engagement with people.

When you extend this thinking to other examples, as in public policy or global relations, it becomes increasingly clear that you cannot approach these situations through a control perspective. Many people in authority positions have learned how to control others in certain scenarios, getting what they want because they can demand it. When they encounter a situation that is more in need of influence, they typically will try to extend their power, either by controlling resources or by maneuvering to gain more authority. The belief in this approach is that power creates change in others, simply because we want it or we will it. I believe, however, that we never have that much power over others and that, at worst, it is an indignity to other humans to try to control them; at best, it is just a waste of effort.

This approach to inspirational leadership puts individual choice at the forefront. While you may choose a compelling direction for your life, there is no reason that others will follow it, except that they want to. In organization contexts, there are practices that work to compel people to comply with policies and practices. If you look at the research, you will find that committed people will consistently outperform compliant people. As a leader, you want people to see the merit in your direction and then willingly choose to place their efforts in that direction. Leadership and change are inextricably coupled. While many people may not think of a change as going a new direction, it absolutely is. If people were already there, you would not need to lead them. It is always a requirement that people change behaviors in order to accomplish different outcomes.

PEOPLE CHANGE BECAUSE THEY CHOOSE TO CHANGE

In reality, no one really knows how to control change in complex human systems—or in individual human beings for that matter. Humans are not very good at intentionally and systematically changing other people's beliefs, practices, or habits, particularly en masse in an organizational setting. At a fundamental level, the term *managed change* can be an oxymoron.

The pages of history chronicle a cavalcade of change efforts and every one of these is accompanied by stories of clever people who chose to resist in a multitude of ways. Change in human systems is complex, but it still boils down to individuals deciding to change. Starting from the position that people only change if they so choose certainly simplifies the matter for all concerned. *Ten Tasks of Change* documents this approach, one of the central concepts being the "change equation."

At the same time, we should take note of certain things that tend to be true about humans. It can be said that people *do* change, readily and often. People really don't resist change itself; rather, in most situations they resist being changed from outside. Change can usually be divided into two domains: that which drives change from a perspective of imposition, and that which cultivates change from a perspective of collaboration. The fundamentals of change seem to hold true across either perspective, but the outcomes can be radically different

THE CHANGE EQUATION

$$C = D \times V \times F > PC$$

Figure 3.1: The Change Equation

The change equation ($C = D \times V \times F > PC$) is used as a diagnostic tool for change work.

- C is the amount of change people will accomplish.
- D is their dissatisfaction with the status quo.
- V is their vision of a preferred future.
- F is their clarity about the first steps in how to go about changing.
- PC is their perceived costs of changing (personal cost and to people or institutions they care about) that reflects the potential for resistance to a change.

There is nothing truly mathematic about this equation, but we present it this way to illustrate how the different aspects work together. You can create change by altering the status of any of these points, but interventions in different parts create different sorts of outcomes overall. The other reason for depicting this mathematically is to illustrate the impact of having none (or very little) of a particular aspect. If any of the factors of D, V, or F in the situation are very weak or zero, you will get little movement, as zero times anything is zero. Also, if perceived cost is extremely high, it will drown out weak dissatisfaction, vision, or first steps. This illustrates a relationship, not a calculation. Just understand that if the perceived cost of changing is quite high, then it would take a lot of work on vision, dissatisfaction, and first steps to have people move. At the same time, if you can lessen the perceived cost, change will occur more readily.

As we deepen our understanding of change, we can look at the two elements of dissatisfaction and of vision. We see through the change equation that they are inter-related and dependent on each other. Each has a very different role to play in how we, as humans, engage life and choose to change or stay the same.

DRIVING DISSATISFACTION OR FOSTERING VISION

Change methodologies fall into two major categories: those that drive dissatisfaction and those that foster vision. While you will find similar elements in each, you need to understand the idea of ideological congruence, in which the approach you take to a complex situation actually matches the ideology that you espouse. Major change methodologies are built around driving dissatisfaction (sometimes called "turning up the heat"). While these can drive a lot of change, the overall results tend to be unpredictable and inconsistent across the organization. There is a well-known story about an oil rig in the North Sea that caught fire, and in the midst of this, one of the workers jumped off of the platform into the sea at night. If you're familiar with the North Sea, you know it is tremendously cold and rough, and that life expectancy, once in that water, is measured in minutes. The story has been used as a metaphor for change in organizations, as to the need to create a "burning platform" to get people to move very quickly.

If you look at this scenario through the change equation, you will see that before the fire, the dissatisfaction was probably reasonably low and the vision unknown; there was no need for first steps, as the perceived cost of going anywhere at that moment was very high. There was little probability of change. However, when the platform erupted into flames and the person's life was at immediate risk, the dissatisfaction with the current state became extremely high. There was not a lot of time to do vision creation, but one quick option became leaping over the side of the oil rig and into the North Sea below. First steps followed quickly, and over the side he went.

The problem with driving dissatisfaction in a group is that you get change, but it is undifferentiated and unpredictable. Without a cohesive sense of vision that is shared across the organization, each person creates his own vision and his own first steps. Each person creates change in her own direction. Very often, this sort of change devolves into "every man for himself," and the system suffers greatly for it.

The most effective change efforts put vision in the center and work to align people around that direction. By working to achieve a unified sense of shared vision, you create a collective movement toward a shared aspiration. As this sense of vision increases and becomes more compelling, it tends to create its own sense of dissatisfaction among its constituents. Concurrently, given time, perceived cost often lowers on its own, and frequently, the perceived cost of staying the same goes up. You begin to build a collective consciousness toward the desired state, and the system begins to change naturally.

You can easily see how certain aspects of each change approach might seem as if they overlap, and we know that all four components are necessary for any change to occur. It becomes a difference of which one we use first. This becomes a real differentiator of inspirational leadership. When you stay with a vision, with a focus on what is possible and what you hope to create, you can connect to the generative and creative nature of people. You engage consciousness and create a journey that people will take together.

Leading through inspiration and vision puts the humanity of your position in the forefront. When people can hear your story, see your commitment in action, and feel your passion, you have the required first connection. You will begin to open people to your vision through this. While a burning platform can create an exciting metaphor for change, in truth you are not leading people over the side and into the North Sea, nor should you want to. You are creating positive and compelling circumstances in which people can thrive and prosper.

PERCEPTION—WHAT MEETS THE EYE

To deepen our understanding of how we work change in groups of people, we must begin by realizing that we are first dealing with perceptions. People listen to us talk about vision, but they see and hear it through a filter of experience. There is a huge amount of inference that occurs between our thoughts and another person's understanding of those thoughts. Each aspect of the change equation goes through this filtering of reality. Once we realize how this works, we can understand the importance of the efforts involved in working with people's perceptions. To do this, let's take a moment to look at how our brains process perceptions.

If we think of the brain as a number of different functions rather than a single entity, we can get a different idea of how it performs as a system. Each of the different functional areas has a role that it carries out somewhat independently of the others, but each can be highly influenced by the other areas. Some areas can play dominant roles at times, and some can completely overshadow the other functional areas during critical times.

For instance, our visual cortex is constantly working to translate into meaningful patterns all of the sensory data coming from the eyes. It does a phenomenal job of smoothing out incomplete pictures and filling in missing information. We do not even know it is happening. Here is an example of a constructed reality: Our retina does not have any sensory cells, or rods and cones, at the point where the optic nerve connects through the back of the eye. That means that we all have a literal blind spot in both eyes that carries no visual information. We are not aware of that spot, and we don't notice a gap in images when we look at a solid wall, even when we only use one eye.

Let's take a moment and demonstrate that you have a blind spot. Close your right eye and look at the plus sign. Move the page nearer and farther from your face, holding your head still and fixing your gaze on the plus sign. At some point, the dot will disappear.

●   +

Figure 3.2: Test for Blind Spot

When the dot disappeared, what remained? Did you see a gap, or did the page seem to continue unbroken, having been filled in by the color of the paper surrounding the spot? Most people will experience the spot as being filled in, suddenly disappearing, only to reappear when the distance changes.

What is the significance between this and leadership? Quite simply, we need to be aware of the many perceptual distortions that the brain offers in the interest of generating meaning. This is only a small example of the amount of inference occurring in our brains every moment of every day. We are functioning through a series of perceptual filters, all of which are designed to serve our highest good and to provide meaningful focus around what we find to be important.

As stated, the visual cortex is working to take all of this disparate visual information and create an image of a coherent whole. We add to that by "teaching" our brains, over time, which coherent wholes we are interested in seeing. Our perception is largely focused on that which we have chosen to see over time. This part of the brain is fulfilling this function every moment of every day and will continue finding the same images until another part of the brain intervenes to offer something new.

This is called "reticular activation," and it is part of how the parts of the brain function as a highly complex and interdependent system to create human consciousness and behavior. If something becomes important in the environment and you set your consciousness toward finding it, you will. Furthermore, you will train your reticular activation system to find that particular coherent whole, in the midst of all of that sensory data, and show it to you every time it presents itself. Knowing that the brain fills in for any missing data, it will even show you patterns that only seem to be there, based on sketchy or incomplete information. To top that off, you will not know the difference, unless some other part of the brain intervenes and creates an experiment to authenticate the image. As an example, once you know a person, you will recognize him even when you only see a part of him, such as when his face is turned away from you. The actual data reaching your eye is incomplete, but your brain fills in the rest of the picture and identifies the image as the person you know. Now, you might call out to that person or touch him on the arm to get him to turn toward you. At that point, your brain has come up with a strategy to validate (or invalidate) your perception.

We can extend this understanding of visual perception to more complex patterns. We do not just see a person's face; we see his or her face in motion, full of energy and complex muscle patterns created by differential tensions. It is constantly in motion, and it changes every microsecond or so. However, we more often tend to see very broad inferential evaluations. When we look at a person's face, we might describe what we see as "angry" or "pretty" or "sad." These can be exactly correct or exactly incorrect. It is important to us, as leaders, to recognize that our brains are filling in the details, and that our perception is just that—our perception.

Add to this all of our other processing systems. This happens with our hearing as well. We have a selective band of frequencies to which we attune, plus many other ways that we pick out patterns from auditory information—we can often pick out the song playing in the background of a noisy restaurant when we cannot understand the conversation of the person sitting beside us. That is because the brain recognizes the pattern of a song and fills in the melody, words, and sounds, turning up the perceptual volume. The person who is much closer, however, and who is coming in at a higher decibel level is not understandable because the brain does not have enough information to fill in the pattern of sentences. Because of the absolute diligence of the brain to make meaning, very often it will take bits and pieces of speech and integrate them into a sentence that the subconscious thinks the person is saying. Again, it does this without our consciousness and can continue until we create an intervention that checks that part of our brain against another and verifies the integrity of our interpretation.

All of the parts of the brain function together as this complicated system, fueled by past examples of importance from our history. This comes from introjections we learn as children, our unique history and experiences, and significant emotional imprintings that occur during our lives. All together, they form a complex set of images that teaches our subconscious how to interpret the world and which complex wholes we find.

As we bring that back to change, it becomes important to think about how others will perceive what we are doing or where we are going. Each person will interpret us differently, and we will interpret each individual through our favorite systems. If we expect people to resist change or our ideas, we inform our subconscious that whatever we see as resistance is a meaningful whole, and our sensing systems will find it. Our personal filters and biases will present an interpretation of what we see, based on all of our own experiences. The people who observe us are doing the same thing and finding their own meanings in the experiences. A complex dynamic is at play, even if none of the participants are consciously aware of it.

As we understand brain functioning more fully, we also learn to correlate different emotions and moods to specific areas of the brain and, beyond that, to specific and predictable thinking results. Because all of these areas of our brain coexist and process simultaneously, we literally function in all areas at the same time. One of these areas, however, will become dominant and will fill most of our consciousness at any given time. That means that every human will have a different representation of reality from everyone else, and we must consciously work with the differences we engage. Just know that these differences are simply a symbolic representation of the world and are unique to each person. As a leader, we need to honor the process that generates differences and not judge the difference itself. By approaching these perceptions as simply processes, we can actually engage people and begin to create the safety and trust required to enter into change.

PSYCHOLOGICAL CONTRACT FOR CHANGE

In any change situation, there is a primal connection between the leaders of the change and the people involved. People look to their leaders for emotional support, and for the clear position of leader in the effort. People want a leader they can trust in many deep and important ways. They crave the certainty that there is a direction and an overall plan. Their desire is to have a space in this new change and an opportunity to have some part in shaping the outcomes of the change. They want to have the freedom and latitude for choice and individual contribution.

They also want to know that their needs are understood and attended to by the leaders of the change. It is often a perplexing relationship, as people will seem to want the comfort of dependence that comes from having a leader in charge of the situation, yet they can suddenly become counterde-pendent and move into fight-or-flight with the leader if their adult indepen-dence feels threatened at any time.

At the root of it, people do not want a change leader to be a boss or a driver; they seek a person who is inspired and committed to a path toward a more highly desirable place. They want a leader who is dedicated and who cares about them as much as they do themselves. This mature level of lead-ership is quietly strong. It is assertive but not aggressive. It is confident but not commanding. It is driven but does not drive others. The journey mat-ters as much as the destination, and we are all in it together. People want a change leader who has committed to much more than the goal or objective. This would be a person who has committed to the integrity of the system, is cognizant of the efforts required to get there, and who takes responsibility for keeping the whole system together and on the same path.

Another part of the psychological contract is the leader's obligation to create safety in the course of change. Part of reducing perceived cost is through making safety nets. A good leader, who connects with his heart and uses empathy, will realize when people are afraid and will work to cre-ate conditions that allow them the comfort of relaxing. People need to be relaxed to be in their highest mental states and their most creative modes. The leader has an obligation to recognize and institute this.

By creating psychological safety, we provide people with the opportu-nity to take risks and change their minds. People cannot effectively examine their core beliefs and assumptions from a place of fear. From this place of fear, they also tend to miss out on their creativity, as their thinking will like-ly be more limited when they do not have an element of trust available.

MANAGING OTHERS

At the core of human behavior, there are two orientations to the world: self-realization and self-preservation. I like the words of others, such as Gary Zukav and MaryAnn Williamson, which takes this to much simpler terms. According to Gary Zukav, we are either in love and trust (self-realization) or in fear and doubt (self-preservation). Our complex range of emotions can be categorized into one realm or the other. Abraham Maslow, one of the early researchers on human psychology, was an early proponent of needs-based theory. He described our earliest development as getting our basic needs met for safety, shelter, socialization, etc. This was outlined in Maslow's Hierarchy of Needs. He ascertained that we started out with basic needs for self-preservation, and then as those needs were met, we evolved into higher forms of consciousness, eventually reaching a state of self-actualization, where these basic needs had little to do with driving our behavior. He saw this as a fairly linear progression, with only some people reaching self-actualization and usually much later in life (between the ages of about sixty to sixty-five).

However, we now know that this is not so linear. After we become adults and can attend to our most basic needs, we can find ourselves in cases where we move in and out of these two modes. With current brain research, we can even see how the brain processes differently between the two modes, literally processing the self-preservation in the left frontal lobe and self-realization in the right frontal lobe. Research shows us that people who operate from their left frontal lobe tend to focus on details and move quickly from one item to another, "hyperfocusing" on one area at the expense of others. The right frontal lobe gives us a bigger picture and provides more options, opportunities, and interrelations than the left. Error rates and accident rates are lower from the right frontal lobe, as this lobe tends to scan the environment more easily than does the left frontal lobe.

As an inspirational leader, we move into a different type of leadership. Rather than focusing on what people do and trying to manage effort, we manage group experience. Inspirational leadership is a practice of leading emotions and aspirations. Just as we have learned to manage ourselves and create microtransformations in our perceptual field, we now work to support this in others. There is no way we can ever control how another person experiences the world—or for that matter, even really understand how they experience it. We can, however, support their ability to see alternatives. If we, as leaders, stand impeccably for possibilities and opportunities, we will create that in the group. It is absolutely essential that we focus on the choices people make with regard to how to interpret and engage the world. This is where we obtain the power of transformation. We can support it, but we can never force it.

PEOPLE CHOOSE WHAT THEY WILL OR WON'T DO

Ultimately, all human behavior comes down to individual choices. When we began this discussion about leadership, we talked about the idea that we are ultimately responsible for everything we do. We can expand that and say that every human is ultimately responsible for every aspect of his life and every action that he takes—a really strong statement that speaks quite robustly to ultimate human power and consciousness. We can extend that to the most basic level and say that we even choose the areas of which we remain unaware.

This frames our position as leaders. People cannot be forced—at least, not for long. We know that we can enslave the body but not the mind. We can use powerful psychological methods of brainwashing to create thought control, but that is only temporary. We can create systems that direct or captivate the attention and influence the thinking of people, but we cannot control the total flow of information or how people interpret it. We just cannot control other people. Besides that, we really don't want to. While many people in authority positions wish they could mandate or dictate direction and action for large groups of people, it is truly impossible to do with any degree of success. It is also completely undesirable to do so when operating through any degree of human dignity.

Human beings truly choose who they are, how much they will accomplish, and how they will engage the world at every second of every day. That is simply a fact of existence. As leaders, we must recognize this and commit to honoring that fact. Unfortunately, many things in life teach us an ultimate deception about people, and we have many practices that are built from the premise that people can be controlled and their actions mandated. We know, however, that although people ultimately may choose to comply with a direction, the results of that pale in comparison to what happens when they choose to commit to a direction that is based on the passion they feel in their hearts.

PEOPLE CHOOSE THEIR LEADERS

The real key to successful change is the leader and the choices that leader makes—the choice to engage, the choice to commit, and the choice to share his or her perspective with others. Leaders create networks of thought, energy, and commitment that drive organizations. One of the big mistakes made in organizations is in equating the formal hierarchy with informal leadership. While organizations hire and promote people to lead, they are only figureheads until people choose to allow them the opportunity to lead. A certain position gives formal power and decision authority within an organization; a formal ability to exert some control function over the actions of the people within the organization. It gives fiduciary and legal responsibilities. It does not and cannot, however, give any connection to the hearts of the people within the organization. The primal connection and the deep association of authority to the amygdule makes it easier for a leader to connect, but any connection is will be because that leader has authentically joined with people through a connection of heart and spirit.

Ultimately, leaders only lead groups if the people give them the personal authority to do so. Leadership is a trust relationship between humans. It is created out of a deep commitment of an individual to a passion and a direction. That gets translated into energy and enthusiasm, which can be felt by others and can tap into their limbic systems and move their hearts. Still, they give that leader permission—and give themselves over to following—through willing choices.

The awesome power of inspirational presence begins to show itself when we realize how much we can influence the reality that we all experience. By managing our own thoughts and intentions, we shape what we notice in the world and from there, how much of that comes to us. We also have the same impact on others—our mere presence can impact the vision that other people have of the world and the aspirations that they hold from that point on. The more that we come from a place of deep inspiration, the more positive a difference we can make on others and on the world.

QUESTIONS TO ASK YOURSELF

Change
- How have I created change? Through dissatisfaction or through vision?
- How have I created psychological safety for change in others? What would happen if I focused my leadership work on psychological safety first, before any other aspect?

Perception
- How have I experienced differences in perceptions between myself and others around me?
- What sort of problems did this create? What sort of opportunities and expansion?

Choice
- If I were not in this job, would the people around me follow what I had to say?
- Would people choose to commit their energy to my causes, willfully and completely?
- Would people stop and listen to my message for the future?
- Would people care about me and my message?
- If I were not in my current role, would I care enough to go where I am trying to lead others?
- If I were not in my current role, would I listen to what I had to say?

Exercise for Advancement

- Think of an important change you would like to see happen. This can be in your home, relationships, work, or anywhere in the world you would like to see it.
- Identify the various groups involved. Go through the change equation with how you would approach each group.
- Write out a statement of vision that has meaning to you and others. Ask yourself if you would follow that vision, and if anyone else did, why would they? Look for how others might see this. Go out and ask three other people how they would see or experience the type of change you espouse. Ask them what it would take to risk that sort of change. Then, ask them to teach you what it would take to establish safety for them if you were leading this change for them. Modify, expand, recheck, and then implement!

CHAPTER 4—
LEADING IN ORGANIZATIONS;
TRANSFORMATIONAL VS.
TRANSACTIONAL LEADERSHIP

*When the effective leader is finished with his work,
the people say it happened naturally.*

—Lao Tse

Your self-definition and creativity is a fundamental of leadership. The ability of leaders to be clear about their own passions and areas of importance creates the opportunity for others to share in that direction. If you are clear about where you are going, others can be as well. This enables others to make the choice of informed action.

After clarity of individual direction, leaders learn to engage others in their direction. They learn to honor choice and support change in themselves and in others. Good leadership makes it both safe and desirable for others to grow and develop. As leaders honor choice that is fueled by inspiration, they can have a very large impact across many people.

To engage large numbers of people requires having an understanding of how an organization holds people together and guides collective action. It is one thing to gather a group of people who have already rallied around a cause and, through your actions, inspire them into collective movement. It is altogether different to engage a stable group of people, as in a work system or large organization, and influence them in that setting. In order to do that, you must use all the aspects of leading yourself, leading people, and leading organizations. Ultimately, you can use natural dynamics in such a way to inspire action in many people.

A TALE OF TWO LEADERS

The following examples of leaders will illustrate the difference between leadership styles that are transformational and transactional. To accomplish this, we will use two fictional executives who will illustrate how these leadership style differences get lived out on a daily basis. For context, both of these are senior executives in a large corporation who have responsibility for business units. They each have seven hundred to eight hundred people in their organization, bottom-line responsibility, and operating budgets in the $100 million range. Both are experienced, highly respected, and are thought of as quite successful in their careers. Also, they are considered as clear in their written and verbal communications; literate in business, finance, and the language of their business climate; and have a solid understanding of the technical aspects of their respective businesses. Both are considered to be equally competent managers. As you read the descriptions, you will get a sense of what it is like to work in that organization and what the overall impact of their leadership must be.

We will start with Aaron, who has had many successful assignments to date. Aaron is considered as technically brilliant and was highly recognized as a team leader, whose teams delivered many new products and services in past assignments.

Aaron practices a morning routine of exercise, during which time he collects his thoughts about the day ahead. During that time, he hears a bit of news on the financial market. As he looks at some radically swinging prices, he looks for key areas that might affect his business or the people in his business. Thoughts of the people involved in his business with go through his mind, with questions about what they might be trying to accomplish or how some of them might be in panic. It reminds him to talk to his leadership team about ways of communicating with their employees to provide reassurance and emotional support for those who might be impacted. He listens to a bit of music that helps to quiet his mind, and then he sits quietly, ready to begin the day. His first thoughts are around what is important to him in life. His focus is on how he wants to live and how he wants to feel, and he spends a few minutes reflecting on the people who are most closely associated with him in his life.

When he arrives on site in the morning, he moves through the workplace quickly but pauses to offer a brief yet genuine "good morning" to the people he encounters. He inquires about soccer games, school projects, and the lives of the people he meets. He also talks about projects that he knows are important to each of them. A couple of the people are concerned about the financial markets. They fear what it might mean to their projects and the stability of business. Aaron listens with interest, sharing his own reactions to the market patterns. He focuses the conversation on what is important to each of the people and to the business, inviting them to remember what they are after and how they can be prepared to handle changes. The message is honest, positive, and focused on what each person can do to continue to be generative. His confidence and optimism is apparent, and by the time he walks away, they feel enthusiastic about how they will engage this challenge.

Aaron moves into his workspace to plan the day. Before arriving, he had spent time with himself. By the time he got into his office space to plan, he had a good sense of what was important today. Now, he makes a brief list of his top priorities, which he will cover at the leadership team meeting today.

1) Goals for business development. There is a business goal of expanding markets, and he wants to ensure that this expansion is done in a socially responsible way. Additionally, he wants to ensure that the managers involved in these efforts are clear about the overall vision and direction. It will be essential that all of the people involved in these areas are working to accomplish that, not just capture the market share.

2) Personnel development plans for the business unit. As the business is growing and expanding, there is a need to optimize the people and ensure that they are placed properly. There are some underperformers who need to be moved out, and some high performers who need to be rewarded and moved up.

3) Current economic instability and the potential impact on customers and employees. As a team, they need to proactively address any real and perceived threats to the people in the organization

and determine any important mitigating strategies. In addition, they will look for opportunities presented by the current economic environment and decide how they can support their people in capitalizing on the moment.

After writing down these points, Aaron thinks about his own physical and emotional state, ensuring that his thoughts and feelings are in alignment with his vision. Then he opens his computer to check on a few key items. He checks for any current issues in the business that he needs to know about and makes a note to check with Sue, one of his project managers, on a key project. He had just received notification about a delayed milestone and thought it important to discuss the issue with her. Aaron wants to be sure that Sue is managing the impact of the delay well and keeping her team and key stakeholders informed. Times like this can be hard on teams, and Sue is typically good at these things. His key objective for the conversation is to ensure that the project team maintains alignment with their vision and that Sue is able to maintain the proper support during that time.

The time arrives for the leadership team meeting, and Aaron moves into the conference room. The mood is cheerful and excited. As the meeting progresses, Aaron reminds the leadership team of where they are going and makes comments that keep the meeting moving in a direction that is positive and creative. There are a few times during the meeting when the technical issues of the business come up. Aaron's response is to ensure that the issue is properly framed with an outcome for success and that it will be handled by the appropriate people in the business. The leadership team is always aware of what is important to Aaron. He focuses on the overall vision and mission and diligently brings people into that direction. His technical competence is apparent but tends to stay in the background during the work together. His priority is to create the vision he describes and make sure that the people who work in his organization move in that direction as well. The leadership team leaves the meeting with a feeling of confidence and assurance in their direction.

Now, we will talk about another leader, whom many people would describe as very similar to Aaron. Also a competent manager, Tristan has had many successful assignments to date. Tristan is considered technically brilliant and was highly recognized as a problem solver in past assignments.

Tristan starts the day with a morning routine of exercise, during which time he collects his thoughts about the day ahead. During the time, he hears a bit of news on the financial market. As he looks at some radically swinging prices, he looks for key areas that might affect his business or his competitors. Thoughts of the turmoil involved in those businesses go through his mind, along with questions about what might happen to the market, the economy, and his businesses profit margins. It reminds him to talk to his leadership team about ways of communicating with their employees to provide focus and ensure everyone is attentive to the detail of their jobs. He listens to a bit of music that helps him to feel excited and enthusiastic, and then he sits quietly to begin the day. His first thoughts are around his highest priority objectives. His focus is on what he wants to accomplish and what he wants to obtain, and he spends a few minutes reflecting on the technical issues that are most closely associated to him in his life.

When he arrives on site in the morning, he move through the workplace quickly but pauses for a brief update from some of the key people he encounters. He inquires about operational issues, capital projects, and the status of business. He also talks about key meetings on the horizon, as well as the golf tournament planned for an upcoming off-site. A couple of the people are concerned about the financial markets. They fear what it might mean to their projects and the stability of business. Tristan listens with interest, sharing his own reactions to the market patterns. He focuses the conversation on what is important to the business, suggesting they remember their key performance targets and any tough decisions they might need to make. The message is honest, positive, and focused on what the business can do to continue to be successful. His focus and technical expertise is apparent, and by the time he walks away, they feel as if he probably knows what needs to be done.

Tristan moves into his workspace to plan the day. Before arriving, he had spent time with himself. By the time he got into his office space to plan, he had a good sense of what was important today. Now, he makes a brief list of his top priorities, which he will cover at the leadership team meeting today.

1) Status of operational issues. Reliability has been a key issue, and he wants to ensure there is adequate focus in this key area.
2) Capital development plans for the business unit.
3) Current economic instability and the potential impact on earnings and operations. As a team, they need to proactively address any real and perceived threats to the business and determine any important mitigating strategies. In addition, they will look for opportunities presented by the current economic environment and decide how they can support their people in capitalizing on the moment.

After writing these down, Tristan thinks about his own physical and intellectual state, ensuring that his thoughts and ideas are in alignment with his role. Then he opens his computer to check on a few key items. He checks for any current issues in the business that he needs to know about and makes a note to check with Jane, one of his project managers, on a key project. He had just received notification about a delayed milestone and thought it important to discuss the issue with her. Tristan wants to be sure that Jane is managing the impact of the delay well and managing the project costs and properly deploying her project resources. Times like this can be hard on projects, and Jane is typically good at these things. His key objective for the conversation is to ensure that the project timeline is preserved and that Jane is able to maintain the proper schedule and keep her people focused on meeting their deliverables.

The time arrives for the leadership team meeting, and Tristan moves into the conference room. The mood is friendly and focused. As the meeting progresses, Tristan reminds the leadership team of their business objectives and makes comments that keep the meeting moving in a direction that is results-oriented and behavior-pinpointed. There are a few times during the meeting when the technical issues of the business come up. Tristan's response is to ensure that the people have an adequate understanding of the nuances and details of the issue and that the appropriate people will handle it in the business. On one of the items, he asks to be a reviewer of the technical solution. The leadership team is always aware of what is important to Tristan. He focuses on the business goals and direction and diligently brings organization structure and rewards systems into alignment with that direction. His technical competence is apparent, as he is an astute problem-solver and understands the technical aspects of the business completely. His priority is to meet the business plan and make sure that the people who work in his organization are rewarded for doing that. The leadership team leaves the meeting with a clear idea of their next steps.

Overall Comparisons of Primary Differences

	Aaron	Tristan
Style type	Transformational	Transactional
Daily planning	Priorities for vision and people	Priorities for production and financials
Focus areas	Overall mission and human capacity to deliver	Overall production and organizational capacity to deliver
Approach to people	"I care about how you are doing."	"I care about what you are doing."
Engagements	Engages with people on a personal level, discussing their hopes and dreams; sharing his aspirations as well.	Engages with people on a technical level, discussing their projects and performance; sharing his observations as well.
Goal alignment	Sets long-reaching and vision-based goals that are inspiring to the people in the organization.	Sets goals that are realistic, based on process capability and that seem to be acceptable to people in the organization.

	Aaron	Tristan
Style type	Transformational	Transactional
Technical orientation	Has technical expertise, uses it sparingly, mostly to recognize talent ability in others. Once recognized, he provides opportunities for people to achieve.	Has technical expertise, uses it extensively, mostly to enhance or adjust the business functioning. Once identified, he uses the information to sharpen business functioning and to sponsor project teams.
Information sharing	Ensures that people have the most access to external information that is relevant to their business and a broad access to the vision that he espouses.	Ensures that people have the proper level of information related to their particular role and a focused access to the goals and performance metrics of their work unit.

After reading the descriptions, you can probably see that the two are very similar but probably lead very different business units. In either case, you would probably describe them in positive terms. The difference between the two is not one of right or wrong but of the overall results each achieves. You might ask, which one meets his business targets? In reality, they both do. Most organization-effectiveness studies will tell you that both styles will get results when the business environment is stable. However, one of them far outshines the other when the environment is unstable. The style illustrated by Aaron offers far more adaptability and sustainability that Tristan's. During the economic instability that affects them both, Aaron's organization has the latitude to adapt positively, while Tristan's would be more likely to suffer because of a dogged focus on priorities set the year before. Ultimately, Aaron's style supports the inherent capability of organizations to adapt to change and respond to external pressures, and Tristan's does not.

THE CHANGE-STABILITY DILEMMA

To understand this, you must begin with the idea that organizations are living systems. They have innate properties that respond to forces for the external environment as well as the internal environment. These responses are fairly well understood and predictable. If we understand these forces, we can quite gently encourage or allow the organization to move in ways that it will do automatically.

As organizations have grown in size, complexity, and capability over the last few centuries, we have had generations of organization designers and management experts dedicate their lives to creating structures through which individuals can devote their efforts and attentions toward a larger mission. These structures are designed primarily to ensure that people only see the part of the organization that they are assigned to engage. This is not done maliciously but rather to enable people to focus on what is considered relevant and timely information. There are other things built in around control and management, but fundamentally, it is generally a safe assumption that organizations are designed to deliver goods or services. That is usually the basis for the interior design of the organization.

There is a dynamic inherent to all organizations called the *change-stability dilemma*. This means that the organization wants to both change and stay the same at the same moment. Every organization has the inherent capability to grow, adapt, and respond to changes in the environment. It also has the inherent capability to be stable and deliver the same things over and over. In most cases, an organization's major charge is to be able to find a product or service that is of value in the world and then to produce that efficiently, reliably, and repeatedly for as long as there is sufficient return. This tends to be where most organizations, especially those with a financial motive, will place their major focus.

As you look at management literature through the lens of the change-stability dilemma, you will see that management techniques have been designed to teach managers how to use these systems to support the stability of the organization. Generations of effort have perfected these techniques, and most large organizations have really honed the ability to be stable, which allows them to succeed through reliable delivery. You will also see a large body of literature, as well as professional practices, in the area of being able to support change in organizations. As in all systems, the ability to stay the same is largely institutionalized and is basically built into the system, while the ability to change tends to be a special expertise that can be brought in when most needed. The literature and practices will also reveal an entire belief set about organizations—that change is hard and must be forced.

When you look at any system and how it handles dilemmas, we can see that the more closely any system affixes itself to one end of the dilemma, the more difficulty it has moving to the other end. In organizations, one of the ways that designers and management techniques have fostered stability is to focus peoples' energy on the factors that support stability and block the areas that support change. This has been done with great intention, in efforts to shield people from distractions and prevent disruptions to their workflow, much as mule drivers put blinders on their mules to shield out distractions and emphasize their innate ability to walk in a straight line.

By the same token, we know that if you focus energy on the areas of organization that enable change, the organization will basically change by itself, without large infusions of effort from the outside. The ultimate goal is to have a balance of energy that allows the organization to change when needed and to be stable when needed. Because of organization design practices, these forces have been minimized or ignored in the system. The belief has been that it is unhealthy to the system to have any focus on areas that possibly need to change available to the people in the organization. In reality, as long as the forces are in balance and in tune with the environment, the organization can respond in either direction, as is necessary. Ultimately, this attention must be brought by the leader. When led from a place of inspiration, people can feel safe enough to choose the proper direction. They can know when to be rigorously focused on the stability and when to relax and move in a different and more appropriate direction.

For a leader, learning where and how to focus your energy in an organization is part of providing transformational leadership. Leaders can, through tapping their own inspiration and sharing it freely with people, engage with an organization in such a way as to liberate the organization to transform itself, when needed. The safety created through leadership can allow the organization to move toward the most desirable outcome, rather than fearfully moving away from something threatening. Many people believe that it's necessary to force an organization to change, but the forces to change are inherent among organizations, and if you understand them, you can design practices that support change, just as we have design practices that support stability.

THE ORGANIZATIONAL WHEEL

Our model of organization is presented in *Ten Tasks of Change*. Based on the Native American medicine wheel, it creates a full representation of the domains of an organization, each of which exists in relation to the other parts. The lines on the wheel show the areas of interconnection, where each system interacts with the others. After studying the model, you can see how a change in one area shows up most quickly in the areas that are represented more closely on the model and take a bit longer to show up in others. For the leader, this can be used in a number of ways. One is as an organization-planning model, through which the leader can conceptualize the areas of his or her organization(s) in ways that might not be possible otherwise. Another way, crucial to our topic here, is to use it as a means of understanding how the leader actually engages the organization, and not the organization chart, the staff, or the direct reports. It is this understanding and consciousness that begins to differentiate transformational leaders. This model shows how the organization interacts internally and externally.

Figure 4.1: The Organization Wheel Expanded from the original published version, Ten Tasks of Change (Pfeiffer, 2001).

The wheel represents five primary areas related to the ordinal directions. Each of these areas, except for the center, has two highly interdependent domains that comprise the areas of importance to organizations. The center has only one domain. Through review of this, you can find every part of an organization and understand its relationship to other parts. This allows you to understand how the forces of the organization function together to sustain it for the long term. We will take each area in turn. The five primary areas and nine domains are as follows:

The North—this represents the wisdom of the system, maintaining the "Why we are here?" and "What we will do together?"

- Alignment with the Environment—this element focuses on the wants, values, and quality criteria of the organization's major stakeholders; the organization's competitive position and the quality of its relationships and transactions with the major stakeholders; the dynamics and future trends in the environment and the implications of those trends for the organization (its strategic drivers).

- Clarity of Purpose—this element includes the organization's defining values, core mission, and vision for the future; its strategic intent in relation to the strategic drivers in its environment and the critical success factors for achieving that intent; its strategies and plans for achieving its goals and the qualities of its core products in relation to those strategies and plans.

The East—this represents the ingenuity of the system, maintaining the information of how we will accomplish our mission and who will do what.

- Core Technical System—this element covers the input and output requirements of the transformation processes that produce the organization's core products; its technologies and practices for controlling the variance in those processes; the information, knowledge, skills, capabilities, and issue-resolution practices required to operate, maintain, and manage contingencies and upgrade those processes to match the demands and dynamics of the environment.
- Human Organization—this element contains the organization's role structure, processes, boundary locations, and network of relationships for accomplishing and supporting the core transformation process, dealing with the environment, supporting the people, and adapting to the future.

The South—this represents the community of the system, maintaining the information of who we are and how things get done around here.

- The People—this element includes beliefs, attitudes, and values of those who populate the human system; their knowledge, skills, and capabilities; their culture, personalities, and diversity; their career expectations; their quality of work-life expectations; their support needs.

- The Enabling Support Systems—this element contains the organization's technical and human-process support systems; information systems; maintenance and supply systems; systems for developing personal and organizational effectiveness; access, control, and authority-allocation processes.

The East—this represents the stories of the system, maintaining the information of what we did and what we did with everything we acquired together.

- Performance Measurement System—this element focuses on measurement and assessment of outcomes and behaviors (business, technical, and human) in relation to the organization's defining values, core mission, vision for the future, strategic intent, and the strategies and plans for achieving its goals.
- Reward Allocation System—this element addresses the distribution of the benefits of participation among the stakeholders in the enterprise (external and internal); the processes for allocating and distributing those benefits and the relationship between rewards and performance.

The Center—this represents the integration of the system, as all of the areas converge here.

- Action Learning—in this element are the processes of applied learning for accomplishment, alignment, continuous improvement, adapting, mastery, and renewal. This capability represents the organization's innate ability to manage the change-stability dilemma.

Whenever we act on an organization, we get a response from that system. Many change methodologies teach ways to impose or force change in organizations, but just like any living system, there are ways to appeal to the inherent dynamics that create change on their own, using the natural energy of the system to change itself. Using the model of the wheel, we can have an easy guide of where to focus that energy. All of the aspects of the wheel are equally valuable and required to have a healthy organization.

At this point, we are simply looking at how we either support change or stability by where we focus leadership attention.

TRANSACTIONAL VS. TRANSFORMATIONAL LEADERSHIP

Looking at the dynamics across the wheel, we can see how the relationship between the domains of systems and reflection create a natural linkage. This is where we can see the design of the change-stability dilemma. The stability dilemma is managed on the horizontal axis of the organization wheel and is the place for transactional leadership. Transactional implies "this for that." In an organization, it is looking at the work exchanged with the environment and the quality of that exchange.

Figure 4.2: The Transactional Axis

When leaders focus the energy of the organization on this axis, they get stability. The emphasis is on delivery and making the process work. Leaders in this mode would spend their time monitoring results and focusing on rewarding the behaviors and actions that are aligned with the core process. These methods tend to enhance predictability and efficiency. This is a very good thing for any organization, and all organizations must have this in place to sustain themselves. Here, a leader focuses on things, activities, and results. The technical system and human organization represent a set of technical skills that enable the core business of the organization. All of it is very important, and when repeated over time, it tends to create the same results.

On the other hand, the transformational leader is concerned with the connection between the wisdom and community of the system. These leaders work to generate the thoughts, conceptual models, and strategies of the system and then connect the hearts and minds of the people who work there with that direction. They are not as directly concerned with the linkage between the systems and reflection. That doesn't mean that they don't care about the stability axis or that it is unimportant; it means that it is not where they spend their time. It is up to the community of the organization to manage these processes, not the leaders. By releasing a leadership hold on the system/reflection connection and empowering the community, they expand on the ability of people to manage and modify these systems accordingly. This unlocks the ability of the system to transform itself.

This transformational leadership is what supplies the ability to change quickly and readily. As stated earlier, all organizations contain the change-stability dilemma and have the capacity to be stable and to change, given the proper focus. In comparing transactional and transformational leadership, we are not saying that one is better than the other. Both are required, and both have their appropriate time and a unique purpose for the organization.

Figure 4.3: The Transformational Axis

The issue for most organizations is that the transactional style has over-shadowed the transformational style. As people focus more on the core process delivery and their performance monitoring, they build more and more capacities and practices that are transactional in nature.

The interesting thing about transformational leadership is that when applied to an organization, it can have the impact of increasing the stability, or it can have the impact of fostering change. When you lead through inspiration and have a commitment to support choice in people, you help connect people to what is important. If it seems more important to the people to support stability at that particular time, then they will. Leaders must ensure that the opportunities to change are present in the system and that choice in the work system is supported.

This sort of informed empowerment allows flexibility and adaptability in organizations. If you think about an organization as pursuing a goal in its environment, you know that the environment moves. Depending on the business and the environment, that movement can be really fast at times. Every organization has its own time cycle in which the organization needs to flex to stay on target with the goal direction. More traditional models had a leadership and management function of looking at the strategy and deciding when it was time to change direction. This is the old maritime model of having a captain on the bridge of the sailing vessel who is plotting the course and calling for all course changes. The captain called for the sails to be set and controlled the technical operation of the ship. In a more dynamic environment, this must be set across a number of people, who work in concert to decide when changes need to be made.

FIVE COMPETENCIES FOR TRANFORMATIONAL CHANGE

What remains is to understand how a leader can engage with an organization to create transformation. Since we are looking at natural forces that already exist within organizations, all we have to do is understand what we do in order to activate and attenuate them. In the upcoming chapters, we will cover five areas of competency that create transformational change in organizations. These are competencies that inform how we engage groups of people and empower them to make profound changes.

Transformation Leaders

- Envision a compelling future (vision)
- Commit to the future (action)
- Set high-performance goals (aspiration)
- Enable inspired action through teams (collaboration)
- Exude energy and inspiration (presence)

These competencies have been adapted from the work of Posner and Kouzes (*The Leadership Challenge*, 1987) and our work on organization dynamics. We have further modified to include components of emotional intelligence that we believe most support transformation and most exhibit inspiration. Within these five competencies, each can be further divided, and individual behaviors and skills can bring this down to a far more specific level, but at the highest level, these are the areas of leadership that make the most difference. It is worth every leader's time to understand how these relate to change and to also see how to use them. Each relates to a particular place of engagement on the organization wheel. Figure 4.5: The Five Competencies on the Organization Wheel shows where each relates. We will explore them in detail in subsequent chapters. From there, you will see how these particular competencies allow you to engage the transformational axis of the organization wheel and support change in organizations. As you work in these areas, you will unleash the innate power of an organization to change.

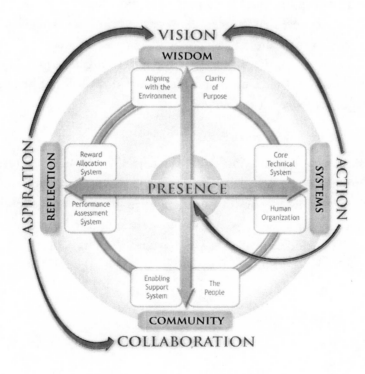

Figure 4.5: The Five Competencies on the Organization Wheel

QUESTIONS TO ASK YOURSELF

Change/Stability
- What sort of techniques have I learned that promote stability in an organization?
- What sort of techniques have I learned that promote change in an organization?

Transactional Leadership
- How do I function as a transactional leader?
- What are my skills, and how do I use them?

Transformational Leadership
- How do I function as a transformational leader?
- What are my skills, and how do I use them?
- How can I increase my ability to support transformation?
- Do I believe that people will make good choices when given proper information?
- Do I believe that in order to support an organization, I need to limit the choices of the people so that there will not be multiple ideas of where I should go?

Exercise for advancement

Using some organization with which you are familiar, identify the most important practices that were supported and reinforced there. Compare that with how easy or difficult change was in that organization. Write out a scenario of leadership that would have supported the transformational axis. Considering all that you have read so far, imagine what sort of leadership would most help you transform yourself and that organization.

CHAPTER 5—VISION: ENVISION A COMPELLING FUTURE

Imagine all the people, living life in peace.

—John Lennon

The cornerstone of individual and organizational change is the ability and willingness of a leader to create a picture of a desired state that is more compelling than the strong reality of today. While some leaders have the ability to literally imagine and see that future, others have to rely on the ability of others around them to craft the ideas of what is truly possible in the world. Regardless of how the ideas are formed, a leader who aspires to create a transformational change must have the ability to articulate some sort of compelling vision and its impact on the future.

This art form involves the ability to use metaphor and story, as well as to understand the hearts and minds of the audience. Using this combination, the leader taps into their hopes and dreams to make the future real. The artist inside the leader creates a mural of the future, with some areas crisply defined and others sketched only as a line drawing. The most effective leaders use their time and energy to engage the people of their organization to illustrate that picture. The leader supports the creative act of allowing each person to "paint his own corner" of the emerging mural. That way, each person can see how he or she fits into the larger picture, and each has a strong sense of personal ownership. By doing this, in groups and individually, the leader can create a powerful draw to the future.

Transformational leaders practice this competency. By that I mean that they both rehearse it and refine it over time, and they also use this competency on a regular basis. Remember, the vision of the future is an image and to some degree an abstraction, while the current state is in the present and can easily overpower a weak vision. The best leaders spend a majority of their time using this powerful competency during times of transformation and uncertainty.

When you look at the organization wheel (figure 4.6), you see that vision fits in the north, as an aspect of wisdom. We consider it part of the overall backdrop of what we want in life and consider why it is important. It is a central piece of living a purposeful life, either individually or in a group. For organizations, having a clear and compelling vision becomes essential, as it creates a competitive spark or a drive toward what is important. Often, you will hear the term used vision/mission in working with organizations. It simply means that once you have seen where you want to be, it can become a mission in life to accomplish it. There is a saying: "If you don't know where you are going, then any road will take you there." For the same reason, if you do know where you are going, it is much easier to chart your path.

DEFINING A VISION

This is one of the most problematic of the competencies to describe, as our language is short on words that adequately capture the totality, or gestalt, of vision. Inevitably, we wind up talking about some aspect or attribute, as the immensity of talking about the whole of a vision can make it almost meaningless. Regardless, we must still be aware of the different aspects and consciously work to expand our perception.

Vision is classically used to refer to a mental image of the future. This is where we begin to first understand how the language simultaneously limits and liberates us. While the vision encompasses the entire picture, sometimes it is easier and more practical to talk about just an aspect of it. However, by focusing on just an aspect, we can inadvertently become convinced that this one particular component is all there is to the vision.

We can start this by simply considering the word *vision*. The definition of the word refers to the ability to see, as in "having sight," as well as defining it as "a mental image that does not exist." More common to our purposes, we use the definition of "a mental image of the future." All of these are useful and representative of some aspects of vision, and it is useful to expand the definition.

Vision, as a term, brings with it connotations of the word from everyday usage. This brings in the aspects of a picture, or visual image, and that it is very often used to refer to the future. However, as we talk about the ability to create transformation through inspiration, we begin to understand that the competency we call vision is one that transcends representational system and time. The good news is that you can still use the term, and it is less important for others to understand the difference. For the leader, though, it is vitally important to comprehend these nuances of vision.

In this work, we strive for a much more robust and varied use, which is more of a definition of what is possible than anything else. We talk about exemplary leaders, and one of the common things we hear is that the person "has a vision," or that he or she can see where we are going. All in all, that is essential to creating positive change. Ultimately, though, we want to live in that vision and have the positive attributes associated with it. We want to get there. The competency we describe here is more than just having a vision; it is having one that you can bring into reality. This allows us latitude to begin to manifest that vision.

To start this, take a few minutes and think about some image you have for the future. (See? There we go.) This can be a work project, your living situation, a creative project, a business you want to start, or anything that you have some energy to think about and some desire to create. This is the first act. In order to create anything, you must first imagine it. Take a minute and write down what you had in mind.

How did you describe what you wanted? Here is a list of ideas and ways that some people describe vision. Did your list include any of these?

Currency: Many people, both in personal and business settings, describe their visions in terms of money. This might be in asset size, type of funds, cash flow, profitability, or any number of ways that they may have experienced.

Quality: Another way of experiencing vision is to describe some terms of quality. This might mean the quality of a product, quality of experience, or some other qualitative term.

Market Share: More common to the business world, visions may be described in terms of competitive position and where the visionary sees himself in the marketplace.

Recognition: This vision is conceived in terms of the recognition you or your business will receive from others.

Reputation: This is very common language in the corporate world and is often used to describe leading an industry. Vision statements related to reputation have been ubiquitous for branding; for example, in the auto industry, Volvo has a reputation for safety, Mercedes has a reputation for quality, and BMW has a reputation for performance.

Environmental: This can have a large variety of nuances, from the environment of your home and living quarters to the environment of the planet.

Community: The emphasis here is about impacting society, from the aspect of the community in which you live or do business or the community that uses your services.

Lifestyle: What will it be like to live within this vision? How will you spend your time, and what will be important to you?

At this time, the Internet search engine company Google has undertaken a number of initiatives aimed at reducing greenhouse emissions. Included in this is a 1.6 megawatt solar installation at its Mountain View, California, headquarters. The company is considering many ways to make a positive global impact on the environment, and according to news releases, there are many other dimensions to that vision. Some talk about Google's reputation in renewable energy. There are also stated benefits in the amount of consumption that will be reduced from the grid, the percentage decrease in their utilities costs, and of course, the number of years it will take for the system to pay for itself. You will see, though, that the forefront of the vision is to make a positive environmental impact.

Of course, the ways in which people describe vision presented here is a short list, and there are probably features of your unique vision that were not on it. In fact, anything that you use to describe the conditions of your life right now could be on this list. This is one of the first places we learn the value of understanding how people create compelling images that move them into a more desirable set of conditions. When a leader begins to work with a vision and starts to explain it to others, it is vitally important to realize that each person who experiences it will fill in the areas that are most important to him in how he sees and engages the world. This is one part of diversity, in beginning to really understand how each of us will hold a different set of values that will then dictate what we place in or out of our vision.

The next part of your description deals with how you represent it. As humans, we experience the world through a number of different ways. At a minimum, we can talk about the experience of our five senses and of our intuition. Each of these offers a different experience of the world, and each of them is remembered or imagined in a unique fashion. We can call these representational systems, as they represent an interaction with the environment. For absolute simplicity here, we will use three of these that tend to be used by a larger number of people. These are called the visual, auditory, and kinesthetic representational systems. Each describes an experience of the world in words that relate directly to that experience. Every person has his or her preference, so the odds are that you described your vision in your most preferred system.

A visual description would include pictures and images of the future. Of course, the very word *vision* automatically has a bias toward this representational system. If your description was visual, you probably described what it looks like when your picture has been achieved. Your language will also reflect that. People who work with this sort of system tend to draw pictures of their futures or create large graphics or signs that can easily be seen that help explain. Likewise, in order to understand, these people like to have something to look at as well.

Perhaps your description lent itself more to stories and conversations. People with a more auditory approach tend to create vivid conversations rather than images or pictures. These people will want to talk about things and hear what others have to say about it. This is an often overlooked area for creating a powerful draw for change. Most very effective leaders use story and metaphor to deepen the appreciation of the situation they most want to create.

The other major way a vision gets represented is in more kinesthetic terms—how we will feel when we have reached our vision. These can be terms like relaxed, connected, settled, and other words that describe an end state. These are common in sports metaphors, as "when we've crossed the finish line." Such phrases provide the more visceral connection to the state and create more power for the leader and the listener. A deeper part of kinesthetic has to do with the actual emotional state that you experience at the time. For instance, we all know what it feels like to be energized and excited. We also know what it feels like to be tired, sad, or depressed. So, in creating your vision, be sure to include the emotional state. In terms of things that can be changed in the shortest possible time, our emotions really top the list. We can change the way we are feeling basically at will, once we have learned how to access these states and how to anchor them in our bodies.

Given that, it is important to expand your description of your vision to include the major representational systems—first for yourself, then for others. Truly understanding a vision means you have mastered what it looks like, sounds like, feels like, smells like, and tastes like. You will understand how this will impact you from an emotional perspective. Of course, it is almost a given that whatever vision you create will be filled with positive emotions, but it is worth thinking about how this new situation will handle problems and allow the most positive outcomes. The more you can create a full representation of your vision, the greater your probability that you can actually achieve it.

The next question for your vision is: "How does it compare to my experience of the present?" Take a bit of time to allow your mind to pass back over the vision you are creating, and then think about a situation that is going on in your life today. How do they compare? Is your vision of the future bigger in your mind that the image of today? Is it smaller? Is it in the same place in your mind's eye? Is it in front of you, behind you, above you, or somewhere else? Are the sounds loud or quiet Clear or garbled? This very important piece of your consciousness is a function of how you have learned to hold an image, other than what you consider to be the reality of today. You can choose to change how you hold this image.

This mental part of leadership is in thought management. We have to learn how to create the types of images that can actually guide our actions, as well as those of others. Through individual consciousness, we guide and shape the meta-consciousness of others.

CONCURRENT STATE OF VISION

As we have talked about making a vision a full and robust representation of another state, we will explore one other aspect of making it real. As mentioned earlier, our best description of vision is actually one of possibilities. While this vision may occur in the future, it is not necessarily *only* in the future. When we talk about possibilities, we think of the coexistence of the vision with the current reality, rather than a seriatim relationship or one of mutual exclusivity.

I think about this in terms of a concurrent relationship and draw the analogy to what I understand of the nature of photons. Photons are described by physicists as being both a particle and a wave at the same time. Whenever you choose to measure it as a particle, it turns up as a particle. However, if you choose to measure it as a wave, it turns up as a wave. Both possibilities and capabilities are present and functioning at all times, but once you choose one, all functioning follows that choice.

Take a very simple example of this. Suppose that you are about to enter a room. Before applying any consciousness, the probability that the room will be dark or light are both valid, and they coexist. However, once you look into the room and choose to turn the light on (or off), the other possibility collapses to zero. Once you apply consciousness, intention, and action, one possibility emerges over the other. However, up to the point of action, both possibilities coexisted.

By the same token, when you hold *vision* as a set of real and achievable possibilities, both your vision state and your current state coexist at every moment. That makes the vision alive in the moment, not necessarily in the future. We have talked about a current state and a desired state. Very often, when presented with this model, people will equate the current state with the "here and now" and the desired state with the "there and then." In truth, when you manifest a new reality, there are aspects that will be in the future, simply because of the inherent delays in systems. Very often, desired states are expressed in terms of outcome, such as profitability or something as simple as a goal weight. Each of these, though, can be brought down to a set of conditions that relates to how we engage the world and produce an outcome. The possibility of living out the conditions that generate the desired state occurs each and every moment. Because it is possible, the vision coexists in the moment. By the same token, your current state has the possibility of existing in the future as well, should you continue to choose that path each moment.

There is one other aspect that makes this a bit more interesting; namely, from a perceptual perspective, your brain does not know the difference between experiencing conditions in the current moment, images of the future, or memories of the past. We have trained ourselves (each person has his unique way) to bring in the images of the past and future in a manner that is different from how we represent the current moment. That allows us to immediately recognize the difference and stay relevant to the present moment with the ability to access past and future as reference. Otherwise, we would be bouncing around in time, responding one moment to a memory from the past and the next to a thought about the future.

In this way, our subconscious knows that it will represent experiences of the future in a certain way and experiences of the past in another way, each different from the way that experience the present, so that we automatically know the difference. Again, each of us is different, not only with how things are represented but where we experience them.

This is a function of our higher-order processing that allows us, through consciousness, to choose how we react to certain events. This allows us the ability to choose responses that are most aligned with the desired state we are creating in the moment.

In fact, because of this, if we actually do equate our desired state with the future, we will greatly diminish the probability of its occurring. Our subconscious is a marvelous mechanism that quickly learns what is important to us, why it is important, and how we will process it. If we train our subconscious that our vision is in the future, it will automatically present any experience equated with it, even if it is in the moment, in the processing manner with which you experience the future.

This is probably one of the major reasons that people sometimes don't accomplish things that they set out to do in life. Holding a vision in the future means we can never get there—because it is in the future. Learning to hold our vision in the present allows us to accomplish it. We must learn to live it in the moment.

Often, people write a vision statement, which is a proper first step to the practice, but they stop there. For our consciousness to begin creating, we have to make the vision as real and as present as our experience of our current state. Moreover, the reality of living out the vision must be more compelling than the reality of living out our current state. Once we have done that, we will begin moving toward it.

In summary, we can define vision as a set of conditions rather than the more limited views with which we began. It is a full representation of the future that is as developed and full as the representation of the present. It is more compelling than the present or the past. There has to be a real reason that it is a *desired* state. Very often, you will see people craft vision statements, but they are missing the key element: they really do not want to live it out. It is not desirable to them. So, in creating vision, we must take that point into account. It must be something you truly want. Once you have created a vision that is full and compelling, and it is something you sincerely want, is will draw your energy and attention and therefore demand realization.

THE ENVISION PRACTICE

Now we get into the competency itself. We use *vision* as shorthand for "envision a compelling future." As we've already established, the goal of transformation is to make things better. Some of the aspects will be in the future, particularly when we deal with large systems. Even with all of the caveats about making our vision real, we still include reference to the future. This also implies that we consider the long-term consequences of what we do now.

In every aspect of our life, we need to think for the future. Here again, the issue of our vision creeps in, as to whether we are literally talking about something that will occur in the future, or whether it is a possibility in the here and now. For leadership or for our world, the very best outcome will be when we can consider our vision of a desired state, see it in the future as having a positive impact on the world and those who occupy it, and bring that to the current moment to live it out to the greatest extent possible. Can you imagine what our world would be like if each of us had the intention of leaving it a better place when we are gone and acting on that in every moment? That would mean that you engage a situation, right now, and imagine leaving this part of the world a better place as soon as you leave. You would be looking for the absolute highest good for each moment. What would you create?

As mentioned earlier, we define a leadership practice as simply what we do each day, or each moment, in the service of leadership. Whether it is conscious, we each have such a practice, and our individual practice delivers our level of leadership to exactly the level we are experiencing right now. While it may seem quite passive, the mere act of thinking about a desired state is the first step in creating. If we think about it over and over, we will create it before we realize it.

IMAGINATION

In order to create anything, we first must imagine it. We have to have some guide for action before we can move toward an outcome. There is a huge component of imagination involved in the practice of vision. We come up with the image of this state, then we use our power to create it. We have to use this standard in conversations and in our planning every day.

Just for now, consider what would happen if you took time every day to think about your vision. You could create detailed stories about what happens in any number of different scenarios. You could make a list of different important events in your life and mentally go through each one of them, using the lens of your vision. You could imagine what the world would look like, brightening up the colors, putting in the right sounds, creating the conversations and interactions you desire with all the right people. You could imagine how the world (or some piece of it) will be left better than when you started. This can happen over and over.

By doing so, we tend to create a full dress rehearsal of how each of these situations will occur with the best possible outcome. We can fast forward our imagination to some future time period and see the positive benefit of the interaction. If it isn't what we thought it would be, we can look back from that point and decide what we could have done differently; then go through the mental exercise again, this time adding to our actions and improving the exchange. This rehearsal, given enough consciousness, can actually become a guide for how we will do things when similar situations arise. The more we rehearse, the better our chances of having these things happen.

This may seem like a lot of trouble or even an absolute waste of time, but take a moment to reflect on this. Do you ever ruminate over events that did not turn out as you planned? Do you go back over arguments or times when you made critical mistakes, reviewing and reliving those events, or even deciding a great argument you could have made or the really good come-back? This, too, is rehearsal. In my experience, each of us has some set of practices, where we consistently mentally rehearse some set of events, behaviors, conversations, etc. Most of the people with whom I have worked, upon examination, rehearsed more combative or destructive thoughts than positive and constructive thoughts. Each of these is a practice. Given that we have choice, which would you rather rehearse?

To illustrate the power of this, let me mention an old research study that involved basketball players. Groups of basketball players were divided into groups, one group given the task of practicing their free-throws every day, and the other group simply imagining successfully making the same number of free-throws every day. As you can probably imagine, the group that imagined making the free-throws improved more than the ones who actually practiced them. There are some very subtle things involved here. Given the opportunity to mentally rehearse, you can choose how well you want to perform. You obviously would imagine making the shots, not missing them. In actual physical practice, however, these players built a mental image of making some shots and missing others. They rehearsed errors as well.

This is another reason why people who are very successful in one area tend to be successful in other areas that they take on. They have already learned to see themselves as successful, and so it is easier to imagine that they will be successful in the next endeavor, as long as it is not too big a stretch. It can play out the opposite way, however, such as in learning new languages as an adult. People who have learned to see themselves as literate and well-spoken may have trouble putting themselves in a position where they are now illiterate and can't speak at all. In these times, it can be too big a stretch for our egos to bear. However, if we can put aside limiting beliefs from our egos, a history of success can make it easier to be successful again.

MENTAL MANAGEMENT

This discipline is called mental management. We take responsibility for what we think about and the impact it has on us, our lives, and the world around us. It requires us to begin recognizing the patterns of our thinking, our habitual language and thoughts, and how we tend to limit our experience of reality through the images and scenarios that we create. Through this, we get to create our own set of thoughts and images that eventually will guide our actions and will become the standard for allowing our vision to manifest into full reality. Typically, vision accomplishment is a gradual process, although there are elements that will happen immediately—almost magically. This only takes place when we create the patterns of interaction that represent the dynamics of our vision.

When we dig into these patterns, we often follow particular mental processes because we either have a rule set that is being followed—often by values instilled during childhood—or we have ways that we learned to interpret the world. At this point, we get to go through the actions of reframing old meanings and rule-breaking, where we decide appropriate action based on our values of today.

VISION AS A GUIDE FOR TODAY

How many times has the scene been repeated—an executive or executive team carefully formulates a vision for their company and then diligently publishes it in all the appropriate channels. It shows up in the annual report, on the walls at headquarters, and even in some presentations to staff. Often, this is because they understand it is part of good management practice or perhaps have done so because a consultant took them through a business process improvement exercise.

I once sat with a team that had worked for weeks to understand some deep issues with a floundering project inside of a fast-moving organization. They presented to their project sponsor, who sat somewhat disinterestedly, making lots of notes and occasionally casting glances toward the clock. He even punctuated some of the longer points of the presentation with heavy sighs. The presenter finally came to the topic of vision and explained that the biggest problems the organization faced was a lack of consistent vision. The team felt as if there were any number of right answers to problems but couldn't seem to locate a compelling reason to do anything at all. During the course of this, the executive wrote on the back of one page of his handout and then interrupted the presenter, saying, "No vision? How about this?" He then tossed the paper across the table to the team. The presenter read a brief and ambiguous statement, about six words in all—more like a slogan than anything else. The executive sponsor beamed upon hearing his words read aloud, and he declared that the statement was good. He then told the project team to print three hundred copies, put them into nice wooden frames, and mail them to all those in management of the division, to be placed on their walls. His next words were: "There. Problem solved. Let's move to the next topic."

In this case, the project team worked very hard to get more detail about a desired state, but the executive sponsor was never willing to put any effort into imagining what could possibly be different. Consequently, the project did not deliver much change or improvement, and the system stayed fairly unchanged until the division was closed a year later, and the overall business was spun off into a joint venture.

Transformational leaders use the practice of mental management to create change. It is something that is done every day and creates a guide to new possibilities. It is surprising to see how many people will talk about vision as a desired state but seem quite content to allow it to remain a desire and to continue to live with their current state. Our transformational leaders apply elements of vision to the here and now and will choose how to behave in such a way as to create the vision in the moment.

One key area of personal management is with regard to internal states. Usually, a fully represented vision will include how it feels to be in the vision. In my experience, I have universally seen people define that desired state in terms of very positive emotions. I have yet to see a vision statement that reads "We will all feel dreadful" or "I will be incredibly unhappy" or "My stress level will be through the roof." My experience is that humans, when in their creativity of imagination, move easily and quickly toward happiness, order, and stability. A very simple way of using vision every day is to choose to feel as you have stated your vision at every point possible. This is a practice of ordering your internal state to align with your vision.

At the same time, you can order your external environment to align. Quite literally, if you have seen your future as containing light and airy workspaces, take action to create that to the extent possible. This can be as simple as changing light bulbs or putting windows into windowless walls. Taking large and subtle steps can make huge inroads to accomplishing your vision.

Lastly, transformational leaders act "as if" they have already accomplished their vision. This is the act of creatively stepping into their desired state. They act as if the change has already occurred, and they are just waiting on some slower elements to catch up. It is vastly different to hold a change as "there and then," as opposed to "here and now."

HOW IT LOOKS IN ACTION— STORIES AND EXAMPLES

Here's a simple example: In our story, our fictional leader, Laurence, has taken the stance of moving the business from a technology focus to a customer focus. After getting clear about the vision and communicating it, Laurence turns immediately to the first place change needs to occur— himself. Laurence makes an honest evaluation of how he is currently spending his time, relative to the new vision. He first identifies all the things he can do right away to live out the vision. Then, he identifies all the things he needs to stop doing immediately to disengage from the current state. Of course, he does this with integrity, identifying critical stakeholders and finding transition plans for things that must continue for some time. Most importantly, he immediately commits as much of his time as possible to the vision. From there, Laurence engages employees and others in a dialogue about doing the same themselves. Laurence now stands in the future and brings people along to join him.

QUESTIONS TO ASK YOURSELF

Vision
- What is my vision?
- Where do I hold this vision in my consciousness? Out in front of me? Tucked away behind me?

Mental Management
- What key scenarios would I like to review and rehearse through the lens of my vision?
- What do I habitually mentally rehearse?
- Is it in alignment with my personal sense of integrity and vision? Vision in the moment
- How do I use my vision on a daily basis?
- Have I ordered my environment to fit my vision?
- Have I modeled my own being in alignment with my vision?

Exercise for Advancement

Select an aspect of your life for which you have some sense of vision. Think about what you are doing when you feel that you are true to the vision, and think about what you are doing when you are not true to it. For each state, get a sense of how you feel. Typically, each will have a decidedly different overall effect on your physical, emotional, and mental being.

Go to a place where you have room to walk, and place an imaginary line in the middle of the space. Designate one side of the line as "vision space" and the other side as "other space." Stand in the "other" space and bring back the feelings associated with that state. Then, step over the line, and switch to the feelings of the "vision" state. Practice moving back and forth across the line, experiencing just how fast you can shift from one to the other.

Once you have done this, you will see that it is possible to literally "step into" the state of your vision. Think of three places you will be this week where it would be beneficial to be in the "vision" state, and commit to stepping in during those times.

CHAPTER 6—ACTION: COMMIT TO THE FUTURE

Go confidently in the direction of your dreams.
Live the life that you have imagined.

—Henry David Thoreau

After the competency of vision, the next required piece of transformation is to take action. This competency, combined with vision, formulates the first two legs of transformation. An earlier quote was "When you pray, move your feet." Vision equates to the prayer; action equates to moving your feet. We have to be ready to pick up and go when inspiration strikes. Most of us have heard the definition of insanity as "doing the same thing over and over again and expecting different results." When we create a vision of a more desirable state, we next must take the action to do something different than we have done up until now. When you see a better way, take it. The question is always "If not now, then when?" It is through this competency that we allow vision to move through us and manifest into reality. We demonstrate our commitment through what we do. These two competencies operate as a subset of the five and are the first place that we begin to see the power of transformation as the ability to imagine—and then to manifest.

Action is a bridging competency, which is seen through the interaction of vision (in the North) and presence (in the Center). It is the entire aspect of "walking your talk" and living the life you say you want. Vision provides the draw and the compelling aspect of your desired state, which is most likely compelling to many other people as well. Presence (more about that in chapter 9) creates a convincing and inspiring force for others that will allow people to see what you see. Action is the process of living this out.

ABOUT THIS COMPETENCY

Beyond creating a vision of what is possible, our transformational leaders take their own action to immediately "step into" that picture and begin to live it as soon as they possibly can. These leaders do not stand by and point into the vision; they move there and beckon others to join them. This commitment amounts to the leaders' moving quickly away from the current state to more clearly resemble the picture of the desired state they espouse. They walk their talk and live the image they present. Moreover, they strongly and supportively coach others to do the same. They turn imagination into reality through aligning all parts of their lives with the future.

It is profoundly different to talk about the "then and there" of change than to create the "here and now" of a change. The former puts the change into the future, where it can be contingent or conditional on some other events. The latter makes changing a concrete reality, anchoring it in the present.

Vision and the power of focused thought create a draw on our consciousness. The universe then organizes around that image and begins to create opportunities for it to come to fruition. Once we focus this power, we immediately feel the tension toward that image.

The dynamic tension between a desired state and a current state is like wrapping a rubber band around your hands, then pulling them apart. If you imagine your vision being in your right hand and the current state being in your left hand, you can see how this tension builds.

Once the tension begins, there are a few possibilities as to what will happen. The farther apart the two states are, the greater the tension will become. If it is too far, the band will break and the energy will dissipate. If they are quite close, there will be very little tension between the two, and movement can be very slow.

To compound this, recognize that your current state is anchored in present conditions. Everything in your life has some connection to this state, many in places that may be hidden or really not obvious at first glance. Imagine that your left hand has hundreds of tiny threads connected to little anchors that are set in various places around you. Some of the threads are much larger, while others are almost microscopic and can be seen only through a magnifying glass. Individually, none of them would hold your hand in place. Collectively, however, they provide a very strong network to anchor your hand in place. You can see some of these threads running to everything around you. Then you take notice that they are tied to items that represent how you live your life. They run to appointments on your calendar. They are connected to the people in your social and professional network. They are connected to your current projects. They are connected to your blogs lists and RSS feeds. They are connected to every place that you currently invest your energy and attention.

Now, look at your right hand, in which your freshly formed vision resides somewhat precariously. The threads anchoring this hand are few or none. Imagine how the tension will operate on your two hands. Without further changes, eventually all of the energy you are exerting to hold your hands apart will become exhausted, and the only available choice would be for your right hand to slowly be drawn back to meet the left.

This can be called *backsliding*, or *goal erosion*, or, sometimes, *lack of commitment*. We know, however, that it is simply that the commitment to the current state (represented by the many threads) is very high. Remember, people are always fully committed to their current state, and that commitment extends in many directions. Some are small enough or invisible enough to require support to find and identify them. Some are large and strong enough to require assistance to remove or replace them.

Let's go back to our example of a rubber band. Imagine you have just created your amazing and compelling vision and stretched your right hand out so that the rubber band is straining at the edge of snapping. You can see the band digging into your hands, causing the skin to discolor. You can feel the tension pulling both hands together, but your left hand suddenly stops, anchored by the network of threads and supported by the hundreds of tiny connections. It stops solidly, all pressure suddenly off of your left arm. All the tension is transferred to your right hand. You can feel the pressure moving up your arm. How long can you hold it? How long before the tension begins to draw it back to the current state?

Left like this, the odds are that you would eventually relax the tension and return back to a neutral state. So, what would you do to hold your vision and assure that it was manifested? It seems pretty obvious: you would try to reverse the situation, to immediately create a new network of anchors that are set in the vision or desired state and to release or transfer the anchors that are set in the current state. The other thing that shows up in this example is that the more help you get in doing this, the easier it becomes. All significant changes are accomplished through networks of people and forces.

Now, the subtle but profound piece to notice in this example is that the natural tension between desired and current state is what creates the change. This change can be in either direction, meaning if we set a vision and then release the tension, we basically change our minds about where we are going and return to our original state. The other direction is to actually change to match our desired state. Either one is a change. This dynamic tension exists every moment that we hold a desire that is different from current reality. If we try to force it and overwhelm the setting, we will probably only exhaust ourselves. If we recognize the natural dynamics at work and allow them to function, we can allow the change to happen naturally and actually relax into it. Simply, the difference in thought will create the opportunity to change. By creating new anchors to the desired state and releasing anchors to undesired states, we can ride the wave of change. Some of the changes will happen in big, fast ways, and others may happen in smaller, more subtle ways. Change does happen, though, and it happens continually, as long as we are persistent in the exercise of our transformational leadership. The more we think of this as an ongoing practice, the easier it is to accomplish. Remember the microtransformation. Every time we return our focus to the vision, and take action toward it, and understand the linkages of the vision, we will experience a series of microtransformation, which will eventually lead to some big ones—or even some huge ones.

TRANSFORMATIONAL LEADERS IN ACTION

The idea of vision as a one-time exercise really fades to irrelevant when we exercise the practice of transformation. Leaders who exercise the practice of transformation use vision as a guide for today (vision in action). Their creative efforts are intended to live out a desired state, and in so doing, they leave their lives and the world a better place in each moment. If we think about every encounter we have, every moment of our existence as an opportunity or a choice point, we can see how transformational leaders move to continually align to the vision. Life is simply a series of choices through which we constantly attempt to achieve an ideal.

In the course of daily life, the practice becomes one of constant alignment. This might seem a bit clouded at first, but it begins with your internal state and how you think and feel at any given moment. If you think of your vision as having positive and constructive elements, there are subsequent thoughts and emotions that are connected or correlated to those aspects of our vision. On a daily basis, you will be concerned with how you engage in the moment. At the most basic level, let's imagine that in your vision state, you are living happily as an investor, looking for the best opportunities and most appealing areas toward which to put your energy. In your current state, you have been somewhat uninspired and perhaps even downright unhappy. One of the first practices is to learn how to switch your internal state toward feeling happy and enthusiastic, even though you are not yet living as an investor. You don't have to wait until all aspects of your vision are in place before you feel the benefits. Add to that being able to guide your thought processes, as your self-talk and internal language create most of the circumstances in your life. You must immediately take charge of any thoughts that take you down mental pathways that are not in line with your vision. Take time to understand how investors think. What sort of things do they read? What sort of questions do they ask? What sort of people do they consult? Then, begin the mental discipline of reading those things, asking those sorts of questions, and consulting those people. Rehearse doing these with feelings of happiness and enthusiasm. Lean into the optimism of knowing you are successful and create scenarios of how you will live out this vision in all areas of your life.

In addition to changing our thinking and our internal language, you can change your external environment as well. You can look around to see how you are spending your time, with what sorts of things you are filling your life and thoughts, and change your environment to match your vision state. One of the most powerful ways of knowing what it important is to look at your calendar. Where do you spend your time?

Another key aspect of action is the notion of "acting as if" your vision state was already there. Transformational leaders step into their future and order their lives as if their future was already accomplished. This does not mean to live on fabrication or delusion but to believe in yourself and take action that makes your vision manifest in the moment. You believe that it is true.

When I was working on my doctorate, there were many times that I was very aware of the need to learn to see myself as a PhD, beyond just having a degree. During that time, I looked carefully at the aspects of people with doctorates who conveyed a special edge. One of my advisors challenged me about the idea of having expert opinions. In his view, as well as many others, people with PhDs were often called upon to provide expertise, and were recognized as having some authority in their field. For people who are often leading the field or venturing beyond the limits of established knowledge, they often create expert opinions that are based on their extensive knowledge in the field, as well as some philosophical basis of valid knowledge and solid empirical methods. That gave me great pause to look at myself with scrutiny, looking for my own "expert opinions." The education and training processes that I experienced gave me a very different frame of reference, and for some time, I had the feeling that my expertise and knowledge bases were actually shrinking. At some point along the way, I remember having the epiphany moment, as I was evaluating a series of research projects in search of an idea I had about leadership practices and coming to a point of satisfaction with my hypothesis. I proclaimed to myself that it was "good enough" within certain parameters and specific situations. At that moment, I was confident in my knowledge and the evaluation to the point that no one needed to affirm or validate me. A moment passed—and then I realized that I just had formed an expert opinion. What a feeling! It was fully two years later that I completed all the requirements to be awarded the degree, but I already was living the thoughts of having expert opinions and following the practices required to feel like they were actually valid. Through that, I stepped as far into the picture as I could, and during each day I "acted as if" I was already there, by living out the principles that I saw embodied in the end state. After that, it was simply a matter of time and continuing.

THE CHANGE EQUATION REVISITED

$$C = D \times V \times F > PC$$

Now we will return to the change equation as it was presented earlier in this work. At this point, we will expand on the use of this model and begin to create some applications for action that our transformational leaders can apply. Let's reiterate parts of the equation (and remember, it is not truly mathematical) for the benefit of review.

The "change equation" ($C = D \times V \times F > PC$) is used as a diagnostic tool for change work.

- C is the amount of change people will accomplish.
- D is their dissatisfaction with the status quo.
- V is their vision of a preferred future.
- F is their clarity about the first steps in how to go about changing.
- PC is their perceived costs of changing (personal and to people or institutions they care about), which reflects the potential for resistance to a change.

The three elements of dissatisfaction, vision, and first steps work together to allow movement toward a new direction. The combined energy of these three must be greater than the perceived cost of changing, in order for change to occur.

DYNAMICS OF CHANGE

Let's expand our example of dynamic tension as in the forces exerted by a rubber band on your hands. We will add in the aspects of the change equation, make this a more robust model, and make it more palpable and usable. The change equation illustrates the required elements of change in either individuals or in social systems. The mechanics are the same for either, although the techniques vary, based on how many people are involved. The change equation is more of a snapshot of change, which is like a still picture that you can use as a moment in time to think about how to move forward on any sort of change. In reality, any change effort is ... well ... changing constantly. As we depict in Figure 6.2: The Dynamics of Change, we place the vision or future state up and to the right. We do not include the word future, even though your desired state may actually be in the future. You can see the "F" in the equation—for first steps—is a series of actions intended to move from the current to desired state. At the same time, the PC—for perceived costs—actually works in the opposite direction to try to move the desired state back to the current state.

First steps take you toward your desired state, while perceived costs take you back toward you current state. Obviously, as in any mechanical exercise, the strongest one will eventually win. The great thing, though, is that none of the energy in any one of these areas is permanent, and it can move from one to the other at will. As soon as the aspect of current state that is most strongly attached becomes "satisfied" in the desired state, the energy changes sides. As perceived cost diminishes, the subsequent force toward the current state diminishes as well.

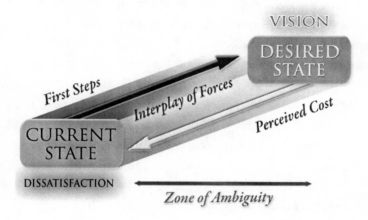

Figure 6.1: The Dynamics of Change

We represent the current state as a better-formed figure, because it has much more density in our experience than does our vision. As mentioned in the previous chapter, we usually represent our vision in less full ways than our current state. We live the current state, so we know it and experience it fully, while the desired state can be more of a notion. In our example of the rubber band around our hands, the network of threads and anchors is part of the density that can tend to hold us in the current state. This figure shows the dynamic tension as interplay of forces, which is intended to show that it changes from moment to moment and from situation to situation.

THE ZONE OF AMBIGUITY

Added to this figure is what I call the zone of ambiguity. This is the subtle part of change that is often overlooked or underemphasized. It is easy to get the big things, such as moving to a different office or changing jobs, but other things go on that can actually be invisible during the process. During the course of any given day, we make hundreds of small decisions, evaluate even more situations, and interpret countless bits of data, all in the service of creating meaningful representations of reality.

When you move toward change, all of these representations of reality are based on your past experience and have more of a subconscious basis in your current state than your desired state. This can lead to automatic behavior that would tend to continuously recreate your past, rather than move you into an alternative, more desirable state. As you focus more and more on your desired state, you will experience times of slight confusion or hesitancy about which direction to move in subtle decision times. Sometimes, you may feel ambiguous and find yourself wavering between two courses of action, both of which can seem the best way to go. These can even become strong enough to create internal conflict that can show up as stress or manifest itself into depression. This is where a constant guide for your desired state can be really helpful. Remind yourself of the direction in which you would like to move, while acknowledging that every part of you wants your highest good, even though these parts may be working off of different standards to achieve that.

FIRST STEPS

The most important thing to promoting change is to make immediate change. The tension you feel against a vision, left unsupported against the weight of the current state, can only weaken over time. This is one of the absolute facts of change. Until you make your desired state more powerful, significant, and compelling than your current state, you will not achieve it. You must begin immediately to reinforce and enhance the desired state, while reducing the strength of the current state. These changes will be both large and small. Regardless of the size, the most important aspect is that the changes need to be intentional. You need to start moving your anchors and attachments.

We often talk about three areas of change when we begin planning our first steps. We can take out a piece of paper, review the way we typically spend our time, and create three lists—what we will you start doing, stop doing, and keep doing. Every change involves some of each. As strange as it may sound, the first exercise of thinking through what we will continue doing has a great deal of merit. Some things in life will not change at all. (No matter which direction I go in my business, I plan to continue brushing my teeth.) This is a place, though, where we can get clever. If we have things that we do without fail, we can use those times and places to remind us of our desired state. In this example, if my vision state has a very positive feeling associated with it, I can anchor that state to when I brush my teeth. You might ask how that would have anything at all to do with my vision of supporting global peace through powerful leadership—the answer is, it all matters. Every moment of every day, we live out the life that will create our vision. When we identify a feeling or a thought that is associated with that state, it will be pervasive through the rest of our life, as long as we have reasonable congruent life circumstances. We anchor the desired state with many small things that will continue into the vision state, and we allow them to help us remember our direction in life.

Next, take the things that you will start doing in your life. Look for things that are within your control and that you can just start doing. In many cases, this is very simple—it only requires you to put up a reminder and start planning these things into your day. It is very important, however, that you put them into your plans first, before you put in the things that you are accustomed to doing. Now, think about how you can anchor these things into your life so that they happen as easily and as automatically as your current lifestyle. Going back to the example of your hands and the tension of the rubber band, you must do things to anchor and secure that vision state.

As soon as you start putting in the new activities, you will immediately begin to feel the internal conflicts that are caused by the anchors to your current state. You may start spending time on new activities that are in alignment with your vision and find yourself drawn back into existing activities or old ways. This is one thing that often slows down movement toward a vision, and it is a crucial step in creating change.

EXIT WITH INTEGRITY

During times of significant change, we leave many things behind. If we look at the scenario of a person who has a vision of a very different life, but that person continues to live in exactly the same way and stays involved with the same people and the same associations, surrounded by the same material possessions, you can be reasonably certain that the vision state will eventually erode away. It is a natural and constructive part of life to deconstruct the old to make way for the new.

Perhaps the most important part of this step is to take time to recognize that everything we do in life, we did for a good reason. We adopted every single practice and association because it fit some important part of us and served us in some way. At the same time, we all live in a connected world, so everything we have done has had some sort of impact on others as well. People have depended on us, we have had responsibilities, and we have provided services to others. This has all had impact, and it has all had purpose. Our life has been spent pursuing some purpose, and the act of creating a vision that takes us in a different direction does not suddenly take away from the importance of what we have done or are doing now.

As we look at what we will stop doing, let's take a moment to do so in a way that honors the usefulness it once had and the importance it maintained to us and to others. We want to leave things behind in life with our integrity, as well as taking care of those who we impact through our action. As an example, if you chose to leave a job, make absolutely sure you take the time and effort to wrap up all the loose ends and create a solid turn-over to others. Spend a bit of time saying goodbye and complete issues with the people around you. One of the hidden drains of energy, even to the things that you most care about in life, is the unfinished business of the past. Small regrets, unresolved conflicts, and even unfinished projects can subtly drain away important thoughts and emotional energy that might otherwise be directed toward your main passions in life.

It is important to look for natural ends or handoffs of projects or associations. Sometimes this step requires a transition plan, as it is common for some handoffs to take a bit of time. I have seen some transitions take months or even years. Ideally, if there is an aspect of your current state that will take a long time to complete, and it is possible to do so, find someone who can handle the turnover so that you can remove that from your consciousness. However, only do this if you know with full confidence that it will be handled well for you and for all of the people who are depending on the outcome.

This can sometimes present dilemmas to leaders, who have committed to projects or situations with all their hearts and minds and now must withdraw to pursue a different direction. In these cases, the reframe needs to take into account that you can still be committed to the ideal or the intention of the situation without being involved any longer. This taps into the power of no in how these leaders literally say, "I care about that, but it no longer serves my highest purpose, and because of that, I no longer serve by being involved." Continued involvement is a disservice to all involved. It is critical to remove your energy as soon as a new direction emerges.

ACTING AS IF

One of the last aspects of taking action on your vision is dealing with how to personally change into the vision state. It is common for people to feel that they can only practice the change after they have accomplished it. A great example of this is when adults learn new languages. Children usually can easily learn multiple languages because they do not censor themselves—they just step in and start using the language to the best of their ability. Most adults, however, once they have learned the ability to be fluent and conversant in a language, hesitate to put themselves into a situation where they are essentially illiterate by attempting to learn a new language. To be successful, people need to learn by rote. The popular adage "Fake it 'til you make it" really applies here. We take on what we can learn about the vision state and adopt that right away, and we anchor our ability to use that over and over.

There are many ways that we can move toward our vision this way. One major success strategy is to model others who have taken the same journey. If we want to be a writer, we look at how other successful writers have led their lives. We see how they have spent their time and the activities that they found important; then we see if we can build our own life to follow suit.

These early stages may feel artificial and contrived, so it is important to pay attention to these feelings. Think about how you rehearse your emotions and mental patterns. If, through modeling or affirmations about your vision state, you feel like an imposter, you run the risk of rehearsing feeling like an imposter whenever you are in your vision state. That is completely against the intention of this sort of exercise. I saw one brilliant coach allow her clients to reframe their intentions to allow their negative voices to subside. This kept them in a positive state and allowed them to remain in the *tone* of their vision while they were still moving toward it. Let's use the example of your wanting to be a great writer: you might sit and write, struggling to put together a small article. During that time, you might experience a voice of doubt that says "I can't do this," or "I can't write." If that is negated, the fear will go underground and show up later. If it is reinforced, it will come true as a negative self-fulfilling prophesy. If it is reframed, however, to "I am open to becoming a writer," or "I am learning to be a great writer," it allows both sides of the consciousness to be true at the same moment. The part that holds the aspiration to be a great writer can be true and possible, and the part that has no history of being a great writer can also be true. This allows the actions to come from a place of integrity and keeps you in the activity long enough for your system to adapt to the change.

IF THERE IS NO MOVEMENT

If there is no movement toward the vision state, there are actually only two possible reasons: you either can't do it, or you won't do it.

In the case of someone's not being able to move toward the vision, we look to the area of first steps. What prevents a person from taking the first steps? This usually has to do with the following areas:

Structure—there is inherent structure that prevents a person from taking steps toward his or her vision. There can be many different variations of this, but it essentially means that something that has to do with the structure of life does not allow for movement into the new vision. Look for constraints in the structure of life, as well as openings, to allow for the vision state to emerge. If there are no openings, we must create them, usually by removing structure that blocks the vision.

Skill—occasionally, the person lacks required skills to take the first steps. Interestingly, this is one of the least frequent situations and the easiest to resolve. Even in the case of the person who wants to learn a new language, he can start with the fact that he already has the skill to speak a language and to learn a language. After all, he learned his first language, and this skill just needs to be tapped in order to begin learning a new language.

Opportunity—this is a very common reason for people *not* to take first steps toward a vision; they just don't have an opportunity. This is the case when their current state is vastly different from the vision. In these instances, the first steps are much more basic and are simply to create opportunities to live out the vision.

Physical environment—in these situations, there may be a vast number of behavioral anchors tied to physical environment. For this, think of an alcoholic bartender whose vision is to be sober.

After this, we look at perceived cost. These are most often the reasons why people just won't take steps toward a change. Most frequently, there are deep value propositions that are related to risk and reward. In these cases, the deep values associated with the current state make it feel as if change cannot occur. A good example here is the person who wants to change her job, but her value of a good retirement is too strongly associated with her current state.

Risk—sometimes the vision state or the steps required to get there are just too scary or the literal risk is just too high. In cases like these, we need to work with safety nets to allow people some way to move without risking everything. As a leader in change, this is one of the early areas you need to address.

Reward—there is also the possibility that while the vision state carries its own reward, the interim states seem to have little or no reward. In cases like this, creating artificial rewards along the way will enhance people's ability to move.

INSPIRED ACTION *IN ACTION*

In summary, transformational leaders use action to:
- Clarify their vision
- Guide their actions on a day-to-day basis
- Strengthen associations with the future state
- Diminish associations with the current state
- Build skills and abilities for the future
- Reduce the cost of change

HOW IT LOOKS IN ACTION— STORIES AND EXAMPLES

Let's consider the story of Bill, who worked as a builder for most of his life and then returned to school to become an architect, with the vision of living in the creative design side of construction, rather than in the daily act of building. His business had a number of long-term contracts, which meant that it could take as long as three years to transition his business into an architectural firm, rather than a construction company. A year after creating his vision, he found himself at a job site late in the evening, digging trenches during a rainstorm and nailing plastic to the roof to protect the job.

After that, Bill was squarely confronted with the question of when he would begin to act like an architect rather than a builder. On personal examination, he realized that his internal state was strongly tied to the problem-solving aspect of building, and he had not found an equivalent in architecture. He quickly found a number of places where he could reframe this, and he began practicing changing into that feeling of accomplishment during design work. He also looked at his environment. His truck had the large toolbox and racks of a builder, loaded with tools and ready to go pick up materials to keep a job going. His desk was covered with information and journals about building. As a next step, he traded his truck for an SUV, in which he could not pick up materials or carry tools. He tossed the trade magazines and reorganized his desk to focus on Computer Assisted Drawing (CAD) tools and architectural journals. He placed art work of beautiful designs on the walls and focused his attention on his new direction.

Almost immediately, Bill's firm began getting work in the new direction. Some people in his company immediately followed suit and reorganized their workspaces and jobs around design; some others left. Bill changed his contractor agreements, subcontracted some of the building contracts, and in months was fully into his new business, years before he expected.

As Bill went in these new directions, other interesting things happened. He started to relax. He smiled more. It became common for him to spend more time creating designs of his own for the artistic expression it offered. While this business funded his life, he found it funded his creativity even more. People noticed the passion in him, and he was called in to much larger projects, including ones that had broad community impact. Additionally, invitations to parties and social events poured in. He found his life was full and inspiring. Others found his presence compelling and wanted him to be involved in their projects. Also, they wanted to be involved in what he did as well.

QUESTIONS TO ASK YOURSELF

Acting "As If"

- When creating a new vision for myself, what have I required be in place for me to act like it is true?
- How willing am I to "step into a phone booth" and change identities toward a vision?

Dynamics of Change

- How do I strengthen anchors associated with my vision?
- Where in my mind, in relation to the current state, do I hold my vision?
- How often do I mentally check in with that vision?
- How do I manage the zone of ambiguity?

Exit with Integrity

- What things have I found that anchor me in my current state and sustain tension with my vision?
- What would it take for me to end my association with these things and release that energy?
- How can I do that, as soon as possible, with as much integrity as possible to all involved?

Exercise for Development

Create a record of how you spent your time recently. Look back on a week, and document how you filled your days. Now, step out of yourself and imagine that you could watch yourself having lived that week. As an observer, look at what you have done, and try to create a sense of mission from those actions. What would another person say was important to you? Think about critical events that occurred over the last month or so. What actions did you take when you were under stress? How would an observer interpret those actions? Now, from the observer's point of view, provide some suggestions as to how the week might have been filled, had you operated in alignment with your vision. Step back into yourself and plan out the week ahead, using those suggestions.

CHAPTER 7—ASPIRATION: SET HIGH-PERFORMANCE GOALS

We are what we think. All that we are arises with our thoughts.
With our thoughts, we make the world.

—Gautama Buddha

This competency takes its place on the wheel as a connector between vision and collaboration. It is parallel to the process axis, indicating that it is related to *how* things get done. Its true significance, though, is in linking the hearts and minds of a community of people through a larger vision that is outside of their own selves. This brings in the power of the means through which the vision will be accomplished, and how we will live and work together as we collectively aspire toward a common goal. This aspirational energy is true commitment to a vision, planning and building how it will become reality through a community effort.

In this competency, we touch on the creative spark that is generated within us when we initially see what is possible in this world. As our sense of vision increases, we will see it gradually encompass more than just the end state and begin to manifest itself in the journey. The concurrent state of vision exists as a possibility in every moment and in every action, and we can now think about how this vision will live itself out *as we are working to accomplish it.*

ABOUT THIS COMPETENCY

Transformational leaders have high expectations. They set lofty goals for themselves and push to be different. Though not necessarily drivers in style, they are always looking to a higher level of performance. Moreover, they challenge the status quo, both in themselves and in others. This is a direct outgrowth of vision. Once the leader sees a new possibility, the next realization is that current types of activities will not achieve that possibility, and new thoughts and actions must prevail.

Here is a key area where transformational leaders differ from transactional leaders. In leading transformation, we must constantly support active and creative questioning of our core processes and practices. When we imagine the future, we only get clear about a very small fraction of what it will actually be like. Consequently, it can happen that people start trying to create a new future by constantly doing what they have always done. A transactional leader tends to focus on stability and predictability and effectively aligns this with people's actions. A transformational leader supports people in aligning themselves with an indefinite picture of the future (although becoming more definite every day), in which they essentially rethink everything they are doing. The best way to find disconnects is to put a real stretch on the system through active goal setting.

A transformational leader spends time connecting people to the mission and vision of the organization. He connects actions and intentions within the organization with what is happening in the environment. A transformational leader will look at a goal, then ask how it can be accomplished in the peak manner. From there, he will work on helping others see these possibilities as well.

WHY HIGH-PERFORMANCE?

Perhaps the question is more like this: Why would you set low-performance goals or goals for mediocrity? There are countless proverbs and quotes with lofty language for aspiration, but this is meant to be far more specific than those. When we think about accomplishing a goal, we have to focus on the way that we get there. In life, the ends do not justify the means. This has been used as a license for many activities and actions that people might not ordinarily do. As a conscious leader, we realize that our desired state is not only "out there" in the future; it also is "right here" as we are living this moment. Not only do we want to accomplish goals that leave the world a better place, but we also want to live in such a way as to feel rewarded and fulfilled as we get there.

In the dot-com days of Silicon Valley, there were a huge number of people who lived a frenetic, project-driven lifestyle. These bright and ambitious people were in a race to capture market share and to be first with new innovations. It was the norm to sleep on their desks or in their cars because the days were so long that they didn't have time to go home. This was truly the second gold rush of California, with people clamoring to be the next eBay, Google, or Microsoft, betting that all of their efforts would pay off big, and they would soon be rich beyond their wildest dreams when their idea went public. Some of them did; others did not. While you can say that they had big ambitions and lofty aspirations, their performance goals were not always particularly high. They had goals that required them to work long, hard, sometimes grueling hours.

The common theme among those who lived through that—or as many of them would say, "survived that"—is that the experience itself took a huge toll. Many people lost a great deal of money, their health, and even relationships in the process—very similar to the gold rush of the 1800s, where the vast majority of the people who set off to work in the mines ended up with less than they started with and were left with the experience of living in a harsh environment, with a body worn from working in extreme conditions for days upon end.

Years ago I consulted on high-performing organizations, during which time I studied a large body of workplace research on organizational performance. The research areas started with overall business success in terms of meeting its customer requirements and stakeholder requirements on profitability and return on investment (ROI) but also included safety, quality performance, and quality of work life. A startling finding was prevalent: people in high performing workplaces typically do not tend to work very hard—that's right: not very hard. I say this with extreme caution, because most people who hear it immediately disagree. Some are outright offended. There is something in this statement that seems to shake the very foundation of our ideas about work, but if you put it in another context, people will immediately agree. Think about it like this: Imagine that you are driving down the highway and see two vehicles, side by side. One is a big Ford truck, and the other is a BMW two-seater. They are both cruising at the legal speed limit, but do you think that both vehicles are working equally hard? Obviously not, as the BMW is designed to be a high-performance vehicle. We can take that to a more human level. Imagine that you have two groups, each with ten people, each with the job of moving a four-ton boulder a distance of ten feet. One group is shoving against the rock widely, trying to position themselves to get the maximum number of shoulders against it. The other group finds some levers and positions them in a way to roll the boulder quickly. Which group worked harder? Which group would you expect had the most time available for thinking and problem-solving during the day? Which group would you expect to have sat down and thought about the best possible way to accomplish the task at hand before starting?

High-performance becomes something that people get accustomed to and actually becomes a way of thinking. If you look at very successful people, you will usually find that they are successful in all areas in which they choose to put their time. This is because they have built a habit of excellence and a worldview that they indeed can be outstanding. Demonstrated capacity in one area definitely transfers to another. Earlier in this work, we discussed the fundamentals of leadership as learning to follow a passion, then learning to put that into the world in a large way. We extend that to include the approach we take to the world and plan to build the habit of excellence *and* the habit of high-performance into our way of engaging the world.

When we take this into more service-focused work, it can become less obvious how one group of people may actually be more high-performance than another, except when we look at a series of process metrics. Even that can sometimes be deceiving or confusing. The best way is to determine high-performance is to check in with the people—it's one of the quickest ways to get a pulse check. If you go back to our imaginary work groups of people moving boulders, what would you expect their physical state to have been, and how do you think they would have talked about their work? Simple questions will give you the answers you need: Are you frustrated on this project? How do you feel at the end of the day—exhausted, energized, tired but satisfied? This in itself will give you plenty of data. I saw a Kenyan runner after he had finished the Honolulu Marathon (26.2 miles) in two hours, eleven minutes. At the end of his day, how did he feel? He certainly felt as if he had done something and felt some tiredness, but he was beaming and healthy. That was certainly a high-performance accomplishment.

There is deep relevance in noticing the way people feel. If they are frustrated or anxious, they will use different mental resources than if they are enthusiastic and excited. The more the dark side of thinking creeps into any activity, the less satisfying the result will be. As a leader, we constantly look to inspire that part of people that helps them find the most optimism and reach levels of accomplishment they did not previously expect.

Inspirational leaders set big goals, then immediately look for the highest possible way to accomplish them. The aspiration is in the outcome as well as in the process. By putting our hearts into this expectation, we will train ourselves to be highly successful, positive, and optimistic on a daily basis. It is what we think about all day. We create an aspiration that gets lived out and generates a level of consciousness that allows us to expand in ways that will surprise and delight us.

If we are what we think about, then think big, and think high-performance. If we look at a goal and expect it to be hard or to take a long time to accomplish (or to barely get accomplished), that is what we will get. If we look at a goal and expect it to be accomplished the same way everything has always been done, that is precisely what will happen. Instead, choose to look at the world and see amazing results. Choose to experience processes that work smoothly and easily. Choose to see timelines that happen more quickly than you ever dreamed. Remember, the Law of Attraction, simply put, is that we get what we think about. Choose to think about living peak performance. The Law of Attraction is that: a law. We use it whether we know it or not—and whether we believe it or not.

THE MECHANICS OF GOAL SETTING

It is worthwhile to talk here about the leader's role in setting goals for himself or herself and for organizations. There are many books on goal setting, and this is not meant to replace any of them. It might give you some alternative perspectives on how to build high-performance and inspiration into your aspirations. Fritz Perls, one of the founders of Gestalt therapy, wrote that perfect therapy involved only three questions:

- What do you want, right now?
- How are you stopping yourself from getting it?
- What are you going to do about it?

In his model, all interventions were based on raising awareness around those core questions and allowing meaningful movement. For our purposes, goal setting is not exactly therapy, but we find the elements to be essentially the same. With this, we can use that particular framework and expand it to a model for setting high-performance goals.

SET YOUR GOAL

It is human to want things. We all do. Where some people stand out from others, however, is in their ability to get what they want, rather than sitting and waiting for it to fall into their laps. The first thing we have to do is to get clear about what it is that we want. I believe that we exist in a benevolent universe, and that all we want is here for us, and all we have to do is ask. I also believe that the key to this is in the manner in which we ask. Many of us are unaccustomed to being able to say what it is that we want, let alone when, how, and how much of it we plan to get. Also, I believe that at an energetic level, we are all asking for exactly what we are getting and most times do not realize it. Part of the asking process, as we talked about in chapter 2, is clarifying the things to which we are saying yes and ensuring that we are saying no to the things that do not fit.

The beauty of goal setting is that it provides an opportunity to clarify our vision in active and direct means. Our goal should fulfill some part of our desired state and allow us to live more directly in alignment with our vision.

Let's go through the process with a number of questions.

What is it that you most want? While this may seem the easiest to answer, it actually requires a great deal of refinement. You need to get very specific and be crystal clear about *why* you want to have this. An example might be this:

"I want to have a net worth of $1,000,000."

Immediately, you need to explore that, with the questions that allow you to deepen your understanding of your desire. The question is, if you had $1,000,000, what would that enable in your life? Would you become philanthropic? Would you live on the beach in Fiji? Would you drill water wells for villages in Africa? Would you start a new company?

So take your answer to this and repeat the process. For instance, if you said "Start a new company," you would again deepen your understanding until you had another set of answers. It is important to continue this exploration until you encounter a value set that feels aligned with your heart's desire.

Now, step outside that statement and look at it from a larger context. Ask how the world will be better when you accomplish your goal. Is there benefit to the planet and to humanity? If not all of humanity, is it of benefit to some? At the same time, will others be needlessly worse off when you accomplish your goal? Does accomplishing your goal do harm to the long-term sustainability of the planet or to its many life forms? See if you can modify your goal in such a way that the most people win as a result of your efforts. After all, it is hard to inspire the hearts of people when there is long-term harm involved. Human spirit loves benevolence, and it shows up in the thinking and creativity patterns of those involved.

How big can you make your goals? It is often worthwhile to expand things to levels that you feel may be just short of impossible, then think about how they might actually be achievable if certain conditions also existed. Think about making the biggest impact, the most positive result in the world. Goals should be the most worthy of spending your precious time and energy to accomplish.

WRITE IT DOWN

While it may seem basic, one of the strongest single steps you can take toward goal accomplishment is just to write it down. Better yet, if you read it every day it is even more likely to happen. However, that is just one aspect of it. Remember, you become what you think about. So you have to be able to give yourself plenty of depth in how you think about your goal.

Make it positive. In this, you must give the outcome a "what is," as opposed to "what isn't." It is simply impossible for the brain to move toward negatives. Even saying something like "End hunger" expresses an absence. While that may nicely denote the end state you desire, it misses the mark as a useful goal. Take a moment to imagine the absence of anything. Notice that your mind can begin to offer up repeated scenarios of what nothing "looks like." Remember that the brain takes in data and interprets it as meaningful wholes, but it can also work the other way. If you give the brain an unknown construct, it will work backward through different sets of images, trying to find a data set that matches your ideal. Left unchecked and without consciousness applied to the situation, your subconscious can potentially come up with an end state that you would not have ordinarily identified.

Write it in the present tense. Say that it is happening now, not in the future. We want to train the brain to accept the reality of the goal, not the possibility that it can exist at some point in the future.

Make it compelling, not repelling. State what you want, as opposed to what you don't want. Do you want to move toward something or away from it? Writing any sort of avoidance goal, while useful, tends to lose some of the power of writing what you want to move toward. In the change equation, the vision state is usually considered the compelling attribute, while dissatisfaction is repelling.

LOOK FOR OBSTACLES

It is important that leaders be honest with themselves. The next question in goal setting has to do with establishing why you don't already have your goal. This provocative step emerges from the belief that you are fully responsible for your life exactly as it is. That includes taking responsibility for what you have, as well as what you don't have. Look at your goal statement, and ask yourself these questions:

- If my goal is truly important, why doesn't it already exist?
- What have I chosen to do with my life and time that has taken me in other directions?
- Does any part of me fear actually having the goal?
- If the goal is truly important, will I stop doing everything else in my life that is not aligned with it?
- If not, what will I keep doing?
- Can those activities peacefully and compatibly co-exist?

Most of the obstacles are in our thinking or are deeply set in our emotional selves. They can exist in our limits to thinking, which keeps us from truly believing that we can accomplish that goal. They can exist in limits to our energy, when we believe that the effort required to accomplish this goal will be too much for us or that it is more than we have been willing to exert. We all have our reasons, no matter what they are. Be honest about the situation and unafraid to carefully examine it. We must take the time to look for what has stopped us already. Otherwise, we are most likely to stay stopped—or at least significantly slowed.

When the goal-setting process is public, it can be an amazing thing for leaders to present themselves in such a way as to let their humanity be known. This emotional transparency can provide the empathetic connections in groups to allow others the same opportunity, to look deep within and find those hidden barriers to success. It is not a sign of weakness to have them; it is a sign of strength to acknowledge them and then work to move through them. We find the opportunity to exhibit our courage and tenacity to others as we acknowledge what has limited our thinking; then, through owning that, we find the path that allows us to move beyond the limit.

Next, create multiple scenarios of how you will experience that goal. Imagine ten of your closest friends and family. Add in a number of people you respect and admire. Create a scenario with each of these people, holding hypothetical conversations and interactions with them. What do they have to say about what has happened? Do any of these conversations surprise you? Are there any that cause you to feel apprehensive? Now add in people who will be impacted as a result of your goal being accomplished. Does any part of this trigger an image that you would rather avoid? If so, you have found another layer of obstacles. Look at this as a treasure hunt—you can only win by doing this. Once you have found your hidden limits, you can work with them. You can build systems that account for the fears you may feel. You can bolster your courage through the knowledge that your commitment is integrated through all parts of your being. After you have had these conversations with yourself, hold your imagination at that point of having already accomplished your goal. Look back to today and give yourself instructions as to how to get there, based on all of the information you have gleaned from your time there.

After all of these mental gymnastics with your goal, rewrite it one more time in such a way as to include all of the things you have learned. By this time, you should have a compelling picture of a goal that is worthwhile and aligned with your heart, and you will have identified the issues within yourself that you most need to manage in order to accomplish your goal.

PLAN FOR EXPANDED ACTION

Now it is time to think about how you will accomplish this goal. What are the most imaginative scenarios to accomplishing this goal? Which scenario would allow you to accomplish it quickly and easily? I like to write out different scenarios, each from a particularly wild way of thinking. For instance, I might ask how I could accomplish this goal at a zero cost. From there, I brainstorm every way of enabling that. I ask other people how they would do go about this and take each idea and see where it leads.

Remember, you are looking for multiple paths, each with the assumption that things will flow freely and easily along the way. Create the concepts of high-performance within this frame. I sometimes like to imagine film characters, setting out to accomplish the same goal. One group that I worked with used to ask themselves, "How would MacGyver (popular as a problem-solver on a U.S. television show) do this?" Or "Would Captain Kirk think this is important?" I also have used successful business leaders or even large corporations as a guide. For instance, "How would Bill Gates do this?" Or "How would Google approach this?" Every one of these requires just imagining what would happen, and it opens the brain circuitry to possibilities that are outside of its normal processing. Regardless of the angle, you will get different answers, and you will create richness in your possibilities.

After expanding pathways, take some time to expand your resources.

- Who will be involved?
- Who will accomplish the steps?
- How will people close to you be impacted?
- What support do you need from others in order to accomplish this?

FINDING INSPIRATION IN THE PROCESS

The process of goal setting is more than just a way to provide focused action; it is an exercise in how we engage the world. The idea of living through inspiration is more than just a concept or an attribute that we want to exhibit to the world; it is a way of life. Simply, the questions we ask during the goal setting expand us into higher levels of consciousness. The excitement and energy that we generate carry us into new places and lighten our own moods. The more time we spend fanning the flames of inspiration, the more positive and generative energy we will create in the world.

In this way of being, the journey is as important as the accomplishment. If it takes ten years to accomplish a particularly large goal, and we spend all of that time captivated by the spirit of generativeness and the image of a positive impact on the world, we will have created a wave of inspiration a decade long that will sweep through everyone around us and will continue to flow for years afterward. The importance is not so much in what we create through the manifestation of the goal; it is what we create in the life we have chosen to build, filled with consciousness and suffused with the knowledge that we can live toward a more positive and ennobling end. The idea that we expect the most out of the world releases energy and liberates us to accomplish more than before. It allows us to have energy left for other things that are equally important. It allows us to work toward an important outcome while having a rich and full life in the moment along the way.

HOW IT LOOKS IN ACTION— STORIES AND EXAMPLES

Some years ago, I set a goal to earn a PhD. That in itself was a pretty big goal, but I added on a few wrinkles. I was working full time, and I did not want to leave that position. Also, the only PhD program that fit my criteria was a 183-mile drive—one way.

Not one to let things like this discourage me, I set about brainstorming how I could make that kind of commute up to three times a week and still meet my other responsibilities on a daily basis. So, I had this idea: I could fly. Not commercially, but myself, in a private plane. That idea added a lot of other complexities. For instance, I needed to have the proper ratings and experience to do this safely and reliably. I also needed a dependable plane I could fly. Above all, I needed to be able to pay for all of that. To accomplish this, I wrote another set of subgoals through which I obtained the proper ratings and licenses. I traded into a couple of airplanes that would get me back and forth. I then left an old bicycle at the university airport for ground transportation.

Before I began the process of commuting, I evaluated the risks and requirements of this sort of activity. I would be flying right over the top of Houston Intercontinental Airport with every flight, during daytime and nighttime both. This would occur year-round, with each season having its particular challenge. I would need to be reliably on time for classes without building a lot of padding into my schedule. My decision, at the time, was to fly it just as a professional pilot would. By then, I was rated as a commercial pilot and had been trained by many airline and charter pilots. It made sense to say that I would consider myself as no different than an airline, and I would set a schedule with weather requirements and operating guidelines to make the flights. I also committed to make the flight under instrument flight rules (meaning I could fly through the clouds and limited visibility) every single time, in order to get the additional support from air traffic control and to be prepared for adverse weather. This was a much higher requirement on me, as a pilot, because it demanded an exacting performance every single time I flew. I thought it would be a bit of a paradox—to strive to attain the level of academic rigor required of a PhD, if I maintained the flight habits of a pasture pilot. They seemed to go together, that one level of high expectations fed the other. In both cases, I was in the habit of expecting the best of myself, and expecting to be able to do things quickly and easily, while meeting high-performance expectations.

After all of that was set, I started commuting by air and bicycle. I worked as a flight instructor to pay the extra cost. To top it off, I finished my PhD a full year earlier than my goal and faster than anyone had ever finished that program, even though I was working a full-time job in a professional capacity and managing a part-time flight instruction business as well.

When I told people about my goals at the time, I invariably received a similar reaction from everyone—usually either a laugh or "You're crazy." My mind-set was one that saw my goals as challenging and demanding but not impossible. As it turned out, flying myself was immensely rewarding and enabled me to accomplish goals I might not have reached otherwise. The surprise in the package was that flying wound up being faster and easier and, at the same time, made the coursework faster and easier as well. The things that were most required were commitment, planning, and consistency. There was a supplemental benefit as well—I had learned another skill that I still use today, and it has served me well in many subsequent projects.

The skill I learned was this: high-performance does not necessarily mean that accomplishing the goal will be harder. High-performance does not necessarily mean that it takes longer. It *does* mean, however, that I expected high-performance. For example, a high-performance automobile not only can get you to your destination faster, but you also can have a whole lot more fun while driving it. Transformational leaders expect things to move faster, to be more efficient, and to have more fun getting there.

QUESTIONS TO ASK YOURSELF

Goal Setting
- How clearly have I set goals for myself?
- Are they documented?
- Do I review them regularly?

High-performance
- What level of performance have I assumed for myself?
- How have I expanded or limited my accomplishments through my expectations?
- Which other people have been brought into my goal?
- Do I have higher expectations for others than for myself?
- Do I have lower expectations for others than for myself?
- Do I believe that high-performance must equate to working harder? What do I exhibit in my life?

Exercise for Development

Think about the most important goal you have. Look at the steps you have in place to accomplish it. Take a few minutes to create an analogy through some object, such as a high-performance car, an athlete, or anyone or anything that represents high-performance to you. How would this goal be accomplished if it was done as that analogy would do it? After creating your analogy, transfer some of these concepts to actions, and re-write your goal, assuming these concepts are all true.

CHAPTER 8—COLLABORATION: ENABLE INSPIRED ACTION THROUGH TEAMS

None of us is as smart as all of us.

—Ken Blanchard

Any time a task is larger than one person, some sort of team is the best structure to accomplish it. Leaders create environments where teams can take informed and creative action. Research clearly supports the effectiveness of team structures (when properly led) in accomplishing all varieties of work. The transformational leader truly looks at how the team's attention and energy is focused. Teams can accomplish great things, but teams also can wander somewhat aimlessly—or worse, can flounder without accomplishing much at all.

To lead a team environment, the leader must think and act with true collaboration. This involves actively building trust and creating emotional safety for communications. In addition to having a clear-cut mission and sense of purpose, teams must have clear, timely, and relevant information and must work together to make decisions and act on the results.

Collaboration fits in the South on the Wheel, and is related to the people who comprise the community of the organization. Leading through collaboration has a number of distinct nuances, as well as a number of misrepresentations. The art form of collaboration is where this competency comes into its own and how it gives a distinct advantage to the transformational leader. When you look at the interaction of vision, action, and aspiration, you will see that these competencies interrelate for a dynamic tension of movement. The next element required is critical mass of people who are also using their efforts toward the same end.

It is a developmental step to begin to function interdependently and to begin to value others' success as well as your own. Steven Covey wrote about this in *The 7 Habits of Highly Effective People*, as he produced a model showing the growth from dependent to independent, then to interdependent. This is also shown in *The Leadership Pipeline*, as it discusses how the progression of a leader through a corporate hierarchy requires him to shift his thinking and values to allow him to support other peoples' success more than his own. To move into this sphere of leadership, you must deeply appreciate the contributions of others and sincerely focus your attention on the success of groups of people.

The other outcome of using teams is the deepening of a shared vision. By getting a larger number of people immersed in a vision, you can work with the meta-consciousness of an organization. Getting multiple perspectives and energy focused on a desire will tremendously accelerate the accomplishment. It also embeds the vision as a reality within a larger social system. This, combined with the ability of the team to take inspired action, can create enormous amounts of energy. As Mohandas Gandhi said, "A small body of determined spirits, fired by an unquenchable faith in their mission, can alter the course of history."

ABOUT THIS COMPETENCY

The benefits of teamwork are widely known, but we are most interested in how to build practices of collaboration that sense the external environment. The importance of this competency rests on two key assumptions: first, that the thinking of a group, when done from a place of consciousness and curiosity, exceeds the capacity of an individual; second, that groups of people, in a place of trust and aspiration, will self-regulate toward meaningful ends outside themselves.

GROUP THINKING

Years ago, I was involved in a series of team-development activities that were designed to enhance the relationship between management and workers in a heavy manufacturing environment. The facility's managers were all engineers and doubtless were among the smartest people I have ever worked around. There were plenty of smart people in the union ranks, too, as well as a great number of people who, on conventional intelligence tests, would probably score about average. At the time, I was deeply into the researcher side of my PhD and was attuned to the ins and outs of conventional IQ testing.

One exercise involved a logic puzzle, such as is shown here in Figure 8.1. We made a copy of the same exercise for each table—tables were grouped with all management together and all union together. The puzzles were cut into strips, with one data point per strip, then distributed among the people seated at the table. The entire puzzle was present at the table, but each person only had a small part of it.

> Sara and her four best friends all enjoyed both their gardens and the flock of small birds that took up residence with them every year. Each of them kept birdfeeders in their backyards, catering to a flurry of goldfinches, cardinals, chickadees, and many other feathery species. They often spent lazy summer afternoons, relaxing in the shade, watching the busy activity of the birds flitting to and fro. This spring, as the friends were busy preparing their gardens for a new growing season, each noted the arrival of their feathered friends. In conversation the following day, the five of them were quite surprised to discover that each of them had a pair of birds building a nest in the eaves of the roof of one of the structures around their homes, and of course, each nesting pair of birds was of a different species.
>
> Determine the full name of each friend, the type of birds building the nest, and where each nest was being built.

1. Lee, whose last name wasn't Ward, didn't have chickadees nesting in her yard. Alice's birds weren't making their nest in the breezeway.
2. Sara Tremont didn't have a shed in her yard. The cardinals were not nesting in a gazebo.
3. The woman whose last name was Edwards had a pair of goldfinch making a nest in her yard, but not in the garage. The robins built

their nest in the eaves of a front porch, but it wasn't Ms. Martin's front porch.

4. The sparrows were not making a nest in Sara's yard. Paula's last name wasn't Martin.

5. Beth, whose last name wasn't Ward, didn't have sparrows nesting in her yard. The sparrows were nesting in the breezeway. Ms. Adams had birds making a nest in the garage.

6. The five friends are represented by Ms. Ward, the woman who had birds making a nest in the garage, the woman who had chickadees making a nest, Paula, and the woman who had birds making a nest in her breezeway.

—From www.puzzles.com

Figure 8.1: Logic Puzzle

If you were to look at probabilities based on individual IQ, there is a very high likelihood that most of the engineers could solve that puzzle individually; there is a low likelihood that the union members could solve that puzzle individually. However, we asked the table team to solve it together. What do you think happened?

The vast majority of teams of engineers could not solve the puzzle as a table team (in fact, during the course of the training, *none* of them did), even though most of them could probably have solved it individually. On the other hand, the vast majority of the teams of union workers solved the puzzle, although most of them probably could not have solved it on their own. The results were not what you might expect. You could say that one group's collective IQ was much lower than their individual IQs, and the other group's collective IQ was much higher than their individual IQs.

To understand the outcome, you would need to watch the interpersonal dynamic at play at each table. It turned out that I could usually tell which tables would solve the puzzle within the first few minutes, just by watching how the people engaged each other. The tables of engineers—brilliant, quick thinkers—would rapidly size up a strategy to solve the puzzle and very often would begin trying to dominate the table conversation. Before a few minutes passed, some would become frustrated and set out working on their own to try to solve the puzzle by themselves. On the other hand, there were tables of union workers who would first look to their associates for ideas and techniques. Eventually, they would start to see the various elements and begin to piece together the solution. The majority of the time, the tables who talked to each other and had some intention of actually solving the puzzle did so very quickly.

Another interesting aspect was that the engineers typically knew how to solve the puzzle immediately and spent no time talking to each other about it. They would move quickly into solution mode (at least they thought so), then get slower and slower as they bogged down in their individual efforts. The union tables typically spent a good bit of time talking about how they might solve it, as many of the people were unsure of adequate techniques. However, once they got the idea, they moved through the solution phase very quickly. Having a number of people looking at the data tended to make connections occur faster than they could have made by themselves.

It is something that you can consistently hear in sports—that teams made up of the best players are not necessarily the best teams. In order to be wildly successful, you must first have a team atmosphere in which all of the people are first putting their efforts out for the collective good. This is always an interesting dynamic, because the idea of absolute personal responsibility still holds completely true. Every individual must feel responsible for his or her contribution to the success of the whole.

SELF-REGULATION TOWARD A GOAL

There is quite a large body of literature on the ability of groups to self-regulate and produce amazing results. A number of academicians and consultants have practiced in this area for the last sixty years. Emery and Trist, in their ground-breaking work in the coal mines of Wales and then throughout post-war Europe, began a way of research that sparked the sociotechnical systems methodologies for work design. While these have been repeatedly demonstrated to have great value, they also show another important requirement: effective and active leadership.

The research studies on democratic work systems show that, when properly implemented, a democratic (meaning self-regulating among members) work system will consistently outperform a conventional supervisor/subordinate work system. If it does not have the required leadership, however, it will consistently underperform the conventional structure. This error state, called laissez-faire (literally meaning "hands off"), often leads to the worst possible outcomes. At that point, human-coping dynamics tend to prevail, and much of the energy of the team gets consumed with interpersonal issues, accompanied by frequent starts and stops and direction changes. Attempts at leadership in these cases are mostly efforts to resolve the destructive nature of these dynamics and in dealing with problems created through them.

An entire series of different coping dynamics can emerge through a disconnect of leadership with a team (these are discussed at length in *Ten Tasks of Change*). For a person who works diagnostically with teams, it is well worth the ability to determine the issues with teams, based on the existing interpersonal dynamic. Each has a structural component related to the organizing paradigm (OP) that has been used during the creation of the team and that is in use through team leadership.

Leaders, however, need different advice than learning to recognize the various error states. In the 1984 film *The Karate Kid*, Daniel asked his mentor, Mr. Miyagi, "What is the best defense against a swinging gate attack?" Mr. Miyagi answered, "Ah, Daniel-san, best defense is … no be there." Properly led, teams will self-regulate toward goals and will actually create their own level of inspiration to function with reciprocity toward their leadership. We want to be able to spend our time in proper leadership. The best approach to team dysfunction is *not* to get there. This can be accomplished through a series of simple and effective techniques and is supported through a clear understanding of how to actually lead the team. With effective leadership, team dynamics are typically strongly positive and usually able to self-regulate discrepancies.

TEAM LEADERSHIP VS. DELEGATION

To note, we are not simply talking about delegation here. While the ability to delegate is an essential leadership skill, it is not the best way to run an empowered team. Most people see delegation as handing off a task so that they do not have to do it themselves. There are many places where a leader does need to delegate some of his tasks in order to better manage his time. With a team, however, we are looking for empowered action. There is an element of delegation, but the energy associated is very different. Here, we want to enroll a group of people to handle a key piece of meaningful work. A big mistake that is often made in management circles is to delegate all of the unpleasant tasks to various people and that often means to a team of people.

You must think of this exchange from both sides. The person delegating tasks may be increasing the quality of her individual life by passing off the unpleasant and mundane things that fill her time, thereby increasing the amount of time she can spend performing more exciting and useful things. However, for the person who receives these tasks, it can create the inverse—a life filled with the mundane, with little time to do things that really matter. There is little equity in such an arrangement and certainly little pleasure for the person who receives all of these tasks. Additionally, the variety of tasks may be disconnected and may simply be one step in a larger process than has a great deal of meaning. If you step into the experience of the person receiving the delegation, his world can often be fragmented, mundane, and unrewarding. He often sees very little purpose in what he is doing with his life.

Organization and social systems have allowed separation of risks and rewards and of effort and success. It is entirely possible to create an organization in which all of the work is done by very low-paid people and all of the monetary rewards are received by others, who are not doing the work of the organization. In fact, this happens every day in corporations around the world. Most companies spend time on their human resource systems in an effort to ensure some equity, but you will still see immense differences across some organizations.

Imagine that you could delegate to a person—or maybe better yet, a group of people—all of your fitness activities. These people would exercise and diet for you. They would spend hours in the gym and on the track, exercising. They would work out, based on incredibly rigorous schedules. They would eat only the healthiest of foods in the best possible quantities to promote health and energy. Further imagine that, through careful design of the systems, all of the benefits of their work flowed directly to you, and all of the negatives of it stayed with them. Even more amazing, whatever benefits you created would stay with you, and all negatives created through your actions would flow back to your delegates, to be handled through their daily activities. Every morning, you would awake feeling increasingly fit. You'd be astounded by how lean and strong you'd become, regardless of what you did or how much you ate. Your life would become increasingly full and robust. You could work however long you wanted, eat and drink as much as you liked, and just get healthier and healthier. Now, look at the other side. The people who worked out every day would get a daily dose of hard exercise and very restricted diets, but they never would feel the benefits of their work. They would awake feeling tired, sore, and sometimes hung over. They would see their weight increasing, and their muscles getting softer by the day. Their health would deteriorate and some of them would develop diabetes, hypertension, or heart disease. No matter how hard they worked, they would not feel accomplishment. How long do you think people would continue like that?

We want to have a group of people who connect to a greater vision—the same one that we are putting forth in the world. Teams need direction, to feel as if they are accomplishing something outside of themselves. A team, functioning in a dynamic environment, is a constantly changing and evolving set of roles. They move quickly, they pass information among themselves, and they make timely and informed decisions. To have an effective team environment, the leader must establish a clear direction and goal (or mission) in the environment. The size of the task must be more than one person can do alone, and there must be real interdependence among the members. This means that if one team member does not do his or her work, the others cannot do theirs either. Conversely, the better one member performs, the better the overall performance of the team.

COMMITMENT VS. COMPLIANCE

A key principle to remember when working with a team is to go back to the principles of commitment. From your perspective, looking at the behaviors on a team: do you see people complying with the requirements for membership? Are they doing the minimum but don't seem to reach out and direct themselves or solve problems without prompting? Do they seem to constantly need reenergizing? If so, you are probably seeing a team that is in the compliance mode. They are waiting for further instructions or are just watching to see which way you move as a leader. They are watching you, not the goal. This is not an effective method of leadership.

Teams want leaders who are committed to them and committed to the success of everyone. They want accessibility and connection. They want purpose. When you can clearly connect them to a vision and allow them the empowerment to make it happen, and when the results matter as much to them as to you, then you can have a committed team. At this point, the team will begin to "own" the mission accomplishment and will come in every day, watching for the success of their efforts, more so than they will watch what you do or say. Empowered teams do not need a boss who instructs them. They need a leader who engages them on a journey, who walks the path with them.

THE IMPACT OF ORGANIZATION

We spoke earlier of organizing principles. There are essentially three that we need to understand in order to provide teams with the appropriate foundation to launch empowered action. There are three primary factors with which groups of people are concerned when they function as a group. (Obviously, these are not the only three, just the big ones.) These factors constitute areas of shared meaning that subsequently are used by team members to guide their actions, either individually or as a group. The three factors are as follows:

Role: This has to do with the role played by members within the structure of the organization. It carries meaning to all the members in terms of authority, power, ability, and importance.

Process or product: This is the thing that the team concerns itself with doing. It can be creating a physical product or just handling a particular process. In effective work design, even product-focused organizations need to have attention focused on the process as much as the outcome.

Values: This is the inherent value set of the organization and of the individuals. It includes ideas about relationships with customers, product quality, safety, and economic return, as well as more personal values, such as equality, human rights, personal worth, and others.

What we find is that all of these factors exist in every organization, but they are held in different priorities within the different structures. One will be primary, one secondary, and the other tertiary.

Primary

Secondary

Tertiary

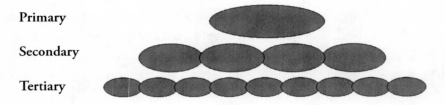

Primary organizing principle is typically one or an integrated set.
Secondary can have more than one.
Tertiary can have many.

Figure 8.2: Organizing Principles

Further, we have found that these factors actually seek a particular order, which is much like the child's game of rock-scissors-paper, where rock crushes scissors, scissors cuts paper, and paper covers rock. Whichever you choose in this game, there is always an established hierarchy.

In organizations, role governs process, process determines values, and values create roles. What differs from the child's game is that all three of these factors are in place at once, and one of them will be selected as most important during the design of the organization. Sometimes it is done consciously, and other times not.

When you consider that we can choose one as primary, then there are three possible structures for teams. We call these OP1 (based on role), OP2 (based on process), and OP3 (based on values).

Basic Organizing Principles

OP1	OP2	OP3
Bureaucratic	Democratic	Community

PERSON (ROLE)	PRODUCT OR PROCESS	VALUE(S)
PRODUCT OR PROCESS	VALUES	PEOPLE
VALUES	PEOPLE	PRODUCTS OR PROCESSES

Figure 8.3: Three Basic Organizing Structures

ORGANIZING PRINCIPLES FOR WORK SYSTEMS: DETERMINING YOUR WORK UNIT STRUCTURE

There are essentially three primary forms for organizing groups of people in a work setting. Current thoughts on high-performing organizations are moving increasingly in the direction of teams. Unfortunately, the word "team" carries many different meanings in our culture. For example, in sports, consider the difference between a football team, a soccer team, and a track team. On a football team, each team member has a particular and often narrow function. The plays are called centrally, and each member carries out the play as defined. If a team member drops out of the game, that member is replaced with the same function (a tackle for a tackle, etc.).

Responsibility for coordination rests with the quarterback or coach. On a soccer team, each team member has a particular function, but those functions are more broad than on a football team. Each member can shoot, dribble, and play defense and offense. If a player drops out of the game, he is not replaced. The team reforms to accommodate the loss of a member. The team is responsible for coordination of their efforts through watching the field of play and doing whatever needs to be done at the moment. A track team has a group of individuals who each compete in his own area. The score of the pole vaulter does not affect the score of the shot putter. They are tied together through their community structure of affiliation and collective values.

It is easy to see in these examples that there is a limited degree of transferability from one structure to the next. The best team practices from soccer probably don't work in football. Part of this is because the games are different, but equally important is that the teams are organized in different ways. In each of these structures, the behaviors of the team members are set by how the team is intended to operate.

In the language of organization, this is referred to as an operating or organizing principle. This is abbreviated OP and can stand for organizing principle, organizing philosophy, operating principle, or organizing paradigm. There are three basic types, differentiated by whether they are structured around role, product, or value. The above examples illustrate each of the three, with OP1 (role) being the football team, OP2 (product or process) the soccer team, and OP3 (values) the track team.

Organization design teams, managers, and work groups who are moving toward team-based or collaborative structures can ease their transition work by understanding the differences between these fundamental structures.

OP1: ROLE-BASED (TRADITIONAL)

This is the most common form of organization used in the past two hundred years. Most people in Western culture relate to this as the most dominant structure in our experience. It has been used in public schools, the military, and corporations. In practice, it exists almost everywhere there are organizations. It has definite strengths and weaknesses—most of us are familiar with both, in some form or another.

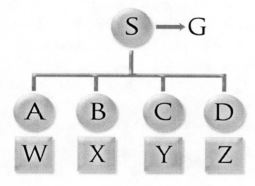

Figure 8.4 : OP1

HOW OP1 OPERATES

The basic requirement for OP1 is one person/one job, with integration occurring at one or more levels above where the work is done. The organizations that first adopted this structure were assuming a low-skilled, highly transient workforce. Through the years, there has been more experience of using this structure with higher skilled and experienced members. The fundamental structure is that every person has a job, which is a piece of the overall requirements for the organization. The structure relies on each person doing his or her job exactly as it is assigned. Responsibility for integrating and coordinating the work is set at one or more levels above the work group.

The members of this work group are typically very skilled in one area, and they handle all of the work requiring that skill. That person's workload varies depending on the flow of a particular sort of work through the group. One person's workload does not necessarily impact the workload of others in the group.

WHAT OP1 REQUIRES

The effects of OP1 are somewhat different, depending on where in the organization the individual member resides. Being lower in the organization has one set of effects; higher has another. The primary role of the supervisor in this structure is to provide integration and coordination to the work unit. The assumption in this structure is that the members below the supervisor need this sort of support and cannot provide integration and coordination for themselves.

As work systems mature and have higher-functioning members, the need for this support diminishes, and the role of the supervisor becomes increasingly one of offsetting the negative effects of an OP1 system.

- Deployment mechanisms
- Feedback mechanisms
- Power distribution mechanisms (delegations of authorities, etc.)

OP2: PRODUCT- OR PROCESS-BASED TEAM

This structure is becoming increasingly prevalent in corporate settings, particularly in high-performing organizations. In this structure, the product or process is of primary importance, and the day-to-day job of the members can only be defined through what is required by the process. These structures assume a high degree of interdependence among the members, and the work done (or not done) by a member impacts the ability of the other members to do their work. Role is much less important in these structures than in OP1 structures.

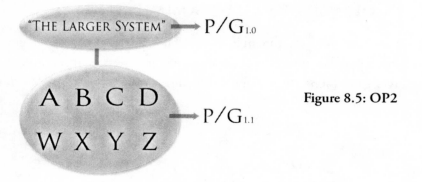

"THE LARGER SYSTEM" $\longrightarrow$ P/G$_{1.0}$

A B C D
W X Y Z
$\longrightarrow$ P/G$_{1.1}$

Figure 8.5: OP2

HOW OP2 OPERATES

The primary building block in this structure is the work group and the complete piece of work that the group accomplishes. Coordination and control of the process occurs in the work group, with integration linkages to the larger system. The size of the group is determined by how many people it takes to accomplish the work of the process. These groups are usually fairly self-sufficient and handle redundancy through overlapping skills among the members. There might be a group member who has an expertise in a particular area, but that person would use that expertise as needed, either to do that work or support others in the accomplishment of tasks requiring that skill. Workload in the group is set by the current requirements of the product or process. The workload requirements are distributed among all the members (by the members), through self-organization.

WHAT OP2 REQUIRES

Multi-skilled and overall process knowledge are integral requirements of this structure. This has a high requirement for self-regulation, based on goal accomplishment, and leadership support through empowering structures and consistent dialogue processes.

OP3: VALUE BASED "COMMUNITY"

This is a very common structure in history, although it has not been widely used in corporate settings. Its functionality is increasingly recognized, and many organizations are working to establish these.

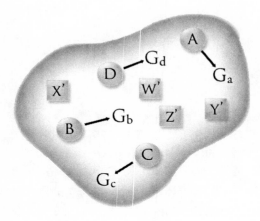

Figure 8.6: OP3

This form is often set up when organization designers attempt to combine team concepts with functional support groups. This is a very appropriate form for groups of experts whose work occurs outside of this group. Some examples are faculty groups, consulting groups, project-management groups, financial auditors, accountants, and attorneys. This structure is particularly useful when the expertise of the members is highly specific, but the support of all the members is fairly general.

HOW OP3 WORKS

An example of OP3 is an early-twentieth-century town. In the overall developing community, the doctor's work did not immediately rely on the blacksmith's work. Each had his particular niche, all of which were used in the overall community. Everyone relied on each other in the long run. They all came together to build their mutual support structures. Schools, water systems, streets, and hiring a sheriff were done together. Occasionally, there were actual work projects in which all members worked together (e.g., building a barn). In short, the common work product for a community is to sustain the capability of its members.

WHAT OP3 REQUIRES

This structure is the most adaptable and has the highest ability to create variety and sustain itself. At the same time, it has the highest requirement for leadership and dialogue. The reason is that, unlike role and process, which are easily seen and observed in action, values exist in the subconscious and can be accessed only inferentially and through metaphors, stories, and examples. Consequently, the only way to maintain alignment within a community structure is through consistent dialogues about what is important.

For a leader, the ability to create community—built and sustained on shared values—is fundamental to leading through presence. While one can say that OP1 is the easiest for a leader, as he can simply lead through directives supported by his positional authority, these are not sustainable and tend to provide the lowest level of performance. In reality, most people like to have individual and group purposes and, from that, to create lives that have meaning and offer long-term reward and satisfaction. Humans are creative and generative beings. The more we can create situations for these attributes to emerge, the more power we can allow to unfold.

LEADERSHIP IMPLICATIONS FOR TEAMS

This is a developmental step in leadership ability. When we start out, following our passions, we tend to be most concerned with getting our own needs met and ensuring that we are successful in our own right. In early years, recognition is important at an individual level, and it is likely to be somewhat competitive.

When creating a team, think about how each team member's involvement will enrich his or her life and the lives of others. This goes back to the ability as a leader to have vision—it is not just about a set of conditions in the future but how we live our lives, and how, as a true leader, we can leave every situation better than before we touched it. Consider how to create an entire piece of work for the team. This means all of the good and bad parts of the job. It is much easier for team members to perform mundane tasks when they know how they fit into a larger context; you will also enjoy the benefits of the greater reward. It is a requirement that they are able to enjoy a complete piece of work, from planning through implementation, and to share in the rewards.

As a leader, the following are important areas for you to address:

- Clarify your beliefs and biases toward teams.
- Identify areas where teams could best accomplish your vision.
- Think through how a team can share in the success of the vision.
- Establish a clear mission for teams.
- Clearly organize and charter teams.
- Develop a clear, shared vision with that team.
- Work with the team for success (not as a team member but as a collaborator for success).

HOW IT LOOKS IN ACTION— STORIES AND EXAMPLES

One example of an excellent use of teams is from a major change in a large corporation. One executive had a vision of an entirely different way to manage sales and marketing, which included how the company would work with a number of smaller distribution companies and several very large vendors. The new model was a complete shift away from conventional methods of working, and it created highly collaborative relationships with the distributors, the vendors, and their own outlets. After spending time clarifying the vision and working with a number of sponsors to expand it, the executive moved to make it a reality.

Stepping immediately into the tone of the new working relationships meant an early adoption of a very collaborative style. The executive brought together a team of ten people, representing the various parts of the organization that would be impacted by the new model. The first thing done with this team was to create a detailed charter, which involved spending time as a team, deeply envisioning as much of the new system as possible, then creating team structures that allowed the group to move quickly and easily.

Next, they outlined a process that would design the new system and implement it as expediently as possible. The internal organization consisted of a few thousand people, primarily distributed across North America. The combined numbers of vendors and distributors was much larger. The team devised a design creation and validation process that would engage a much larger slice of the organization. Each of the ten team members created another team, this one in their area of the organization with which they would work to generate ideas and provide feedback on design issues. They also created an extended network from each of these teams that would engage their part of the organization for communications, idea generation, feedback, and ultimately, design validation.

Each team spent time immersing themselves in the overall vision, deepening the understanding of the whole and simultaneously bringing the vision to the local level. This made it specific to the functional areas and aligned it from the company level down to the work units. After these teams were formed, the executive brought all of them together (about 150 people), along with a number of the major distributors and some vendors. This group went to work again on the vision. It had shifted slightly because so many people had worked on it. It was better, though—it was more complete, more practical, and more robust. It had great potential, and it was truly compelling to the people involved. It seemed that there was something good in it for everyone, and you could identify that down to the work-unit level.

By the time these activities were finished, there was tremendous enthusiasm and commitment to the design concept. Because of the degree of empowerment, the teams were able to briskly move through design steps and create the appropriate models and support systems. The executive sponsor, after seeing the enthusiasm of the initial visioning, used the same forum for each significant phase change in the project. Each time, she brought the group of 150 together to review changes, reconnect with the vision, and create action plans and commitments. As soon as each meeting was over, 150 emissaries went forth into the organization to disseminate the results and work with the series of interlocking teams to create immediate action.

The project finished in record time, with great implementation results. One of the most common pieces of feedback was that it was easy. Very few changes were imposed on people, because they had been made collaboratively during the process, by people who were passionately pursuing a vision. Most important to it all is that the ideas of the new system were transformational. They called for a completely different set of interactions between the company and its customers. The changes were made through people determining the best way to accomplish the vision, which they understood from the beginning.

QUESTIONS TO ASK YOURSELF

Teams

- Who is in my team?
- How do I engage teams?
- Do I find myself feeling openly collaborative or competitive with members of the team?
- Do I find myself guarding myself against a team or opening myself to join?
- How have I created empowered action through others?
- What has been my default belief about how teams function?
- What is the most liberating and empowering action I can take to sponsor teams on important missions?
- What will I do today to accomplish this?

Structures

- Do I develop team structures as role-centered, process-centered, or value-centered?
- Which is my favorite to work within?
- Which structure most aligns with my vision and mission in life?

Exercise for Development

Look at the structure of your vision in life. Work through how teams would look if they were working in each different structure. What would be important to support? How can you create a team or teams who are working with inspired empowerment and shared vision to accomplish this great thing?

CHAPTER 9—PRESENCE: EXUDE ENERGY AND INSPIRATION

The most precious gift we can offer others is our presence. When mindfulness embraces those we love, they will bloom like flowers.

—Thich Nhat Hanh

Connecting all the other competencies is the pure presence that great leaders exude. This is not the same as charisma; it is the ability to be open and authentic enough for people around the leader to personally feel and be impacted by that leader's passion. This is the sense that the leader has a direction and the energy to pursue it, and he is genuinely enjoying the pursuit. It is the feeling of confidence in the intention of the leader. It is the recognition that the leader is indeed charting the course and is living toward it. Through this, people around that leader will also be inspired to take creative action toward the goal of the future. We call this core area "Inspirational Presence." Referring back to the Wheel, presence resides in the center, the place of learning and integration of all other parts.

Presence itself is a by-product of many different facets of your personality, created through what you think about and how you use your emotions. It is an area that is most deeply connected to your spirit and most impacted by ego or fear. When we speak of the competency of presence, we are referring to the life practice of leaders. While many people believe that leaders are born with inherent abilities to engage others, environment and mental patterns shape those abilities throughout life.

The practice of leadership begins and ends with presence. This is how we engage others, but it is also how we engage our own deeper self and understand what and who we are as humans. Here is where the important things in life show themselves to the world. When leaders fully embrace this concept, their presence will show through to others and fuel relationships, ideas, and actions.

ABOUT THIS COMPETENCY

The competency of presence has two components. First, there is the skill of developing a palpable presence—this skill is primarily related to emotional intelligence. Second, there is the skill of being inspirational—this is a more spiritual and connected piece of understanding our greater purpose in life.

Good leaders have common characteristics—being transparent, making thinking visible, and being authentic. If you look at traditional models of leaders, particularly in Western culture post-WWII, you will find a more stoic and directive model. This was the stern-faced leader, cool in the face of fire; he always knew in which direction to go and gave immediate, unflinching commands, with the deep belief that everyone would follow completely. This leader accepted nothing less and gave little back. This sort of driving style has its place, although it is extremely limited. It is also very corrosive for long-term empowered relationships.

I have been challenged on this on a number of occasions, with the idea that someone needs to take a stand in an emergency. That is absolutely true. Emergency situations call for quick, informed, and decisive action. As an example, look at fire departments. During a fire, there is a person in charge of the scene, an incident commander, who is fully responsible for all of the activities related to the situation. He spots the trucks, sends out the firefighters, directs rescue operations, and coordinates every activity. He rarely asks for input (at least, not for very long), and he can be extremely commanding in his style and demeanor. He cares about his people, the emergency, and the best possible outcome. This is an effective use of this type of style.

This type of leadership, however, is basically reserved for the emergency. If you look at life between emergencies, you will see a completely different type of leadership. These incident commanders are part of the team. They have authority and responsibility, but they work with the team members on everyday duties, much like families. They spend hours in training together, building trust and strong relationships with the members of the team. It is the strength of these relationships and the trust that is built through repeated contact that gives these commanders license to direct during emergencies. If the trust was not there, no firefighter would enter a burning building solely on command of a voice on the radio. The firefighters know that support is behind them and that the voice on the radio is a person they know and believe in. Even so, very often these relationships can be damaged during critical incidents through the commanding style, and they require significant interpersonal work after the fact to rebuild the trust and restore the working dynamics.

In a more normal world (for the rest of us), most events are far less a life-or-death issue; they are more related to pressing business issues. We often find that some organizations like to treat business issues as if they were life-threatening. As you know from studying the change equation, this is a fear-based management style that hopes to create energy to avoid negatives or through driving dissatisfaction. Again, while this works to some degree, at least to get movement, it is unsustainable and unpredictable without the deep commitment to a vision. In reality, our lives are only as urgent as we make them. We have the ultimate choice about how we engage events and what parts of our being we live from. We have the choice to live in self-preservation or self-realization. Choose you must, so choose well.

The compelling model for leadership is one in which the leader is deeply committed to a sense of vision and mission and at the same time is human and real. This leader is generous with himself, giving others the gift of their consciousness and providing the uplifting spirit of inspiration. He breathes life into any project or situation.

EMOTIONAL INTELLIGENCE FOR LEADERS

Years ago, people in the workplace often were technically brilliant but had awful people skills. In the past, organizations lived with these people and adapted around them. The likelihood of this happening now is far less. More workplaces recognize that employees must have both technical skills and the social skills of working in teams and of leading others.

Emotional intelligence matters more than intellectual intelligence in most avenues of life. Although surprising to some, having a high emotional intelligence can support developing high academic success. Interestingly, it often works the opposite way for high intellectual intelligence, in that this can get in the way of developing emotional intelligence. Through our physical and social development, we are taught to ignore or subdue our emotional side. Through this, our subconscious learns to ignore the sensations in our body associated with emotional messages, and we short-circuit our emotional learning—hence Fritz Perl's statement: "We must lose our minds and come to our senses."

How we engage others, beyond the mental construct of a vision, is done through our emotional body. This complex set of responses gives us a mechanism through which to connect with others and, in particular for leaders, influence others. The limbic engagement that occurs when we walk into another's physical space—or even enter his or her consciousness, in some cases—is what enables us to take sympathetic action. By sympathetic action, we mean that as a group, we take actions related to an affinity, interdependence, or mutual association. Our actions occur like a jam session among musicians. There is a commonality of key, progression, and tempo, with members connected through the rapport of the music, co-creating something that none of them could have done on his own.

To have this connection, you need to be transparent and authentic. People need to experience the real you and understand how you sincerely feel about things. It requires practice to "thin the walls" that basically hide your emotionality, as well as a great deal of courage to allow yourself to be seen in this light. It is, however, absolutely essential. It requires living through your sensory data more than through your intellect.

Infants live through sensory intelligence and basic emotional intelligence. Our first interactions are through empathic contact with our mothers and then expand to include others. As language development enters the mix, we begin to rely more on the symbolic code of language than on the sensory data of emotions. Further to this, we are socialized to contain our hot emotions and live more through our cool logic. This does make for a more stable and predictable environment; it carries a negative side effect. If you look at early childhood development and socialization through school systems, it is very common to teach children to suppress their emotions. This approach gets compliant and quiet children but leaves behind an underdeveloped set of emotional responses, and it results in a great number of people who operate from an emotional body that closely approximates the skill set they had when they were five years old.

Implicitly, as people age, their hormonal changes and maturity tend to temper these emotions, so they are not as prone to break free as when they were adolescents or young adults. The issue, though, is that most people learn to suppress and repress their emotions to keep them under control. At the same time, it usually does not support a person to have childish emotional reactions showing up in his adult relationships, so he learns to build walls to contain and hide them. These walls seem to serve us from a protection standpoint, but in our relationships, they actually prevent us from getting the sort of authentic contact that will allow us to engage others, deeply and fully.

At the same time, these education processes that created vast cognitive and logical resources tended to teach our minds to ignore our emotions. As a result, many people have no idea what they are feeling at any given time. You may know a person who is deeply angry or worse, resentful, who has bottled up that emotion, ignored it, and let it build pressure in his body. If you enter empathic rapport with this person, you will feel the tension. You will see it in his face. If it is chronic over years, you may even see deep lines in his face from habitually holding that tension.

For this person to lead through his presence, he must enter into a time of emotional education. This is a period of deep personal growth that will impact every area of his life. The good news is that it will make an overall positive difference. This sort of a journey can cause unhealthy relationships to end and can open the door to positive and emotionally rewarding relationships, both in private and public life. To be a leader of other people's hearts and minds, it is a required journey.

The following table is a set of competencies identified in Dan Goleman's work on emotional intelligence for leaders. It is broken into four quadrants, relating individual and social competencies, further divided by internal and external focus. As leaders, we are deeply concerned about the social/external domain, or relationship management. This is where we get to flex our skills and truly engage other people. This is where the power of groups is tapped. This is also where most leaders are immediately drawn to start.

	Internal	External
Social	Social Awareness • Empathy • Organizational Awareness • Service	Relationship Management • Inspirational Leadership • Influence • Developing Others • Change Catalyst • Conflict Management • Building Bonds • Teamwork and Collaboration
Individual	Self-Awareness • Emotional Self-Awareness • Accurate Self-Assessment • Self-Confidence	Self Management • Emotional Self-Control • Transparency • Adaptability • Achievement • Initiative • Optimism

Table 9.1: Emotional Intelligence Competencies for Leadership
Daniel Goleman, *Primal Leadership*, Harvard Business School Press, 2002.

The seeming paradox here is that our ability to work well in relationship management is directly related to our ability in the domain of self-awareness. There is strong interdependence between these four domains—a weakness in one will correlate to a subsequent weakness in others. Of all the domains, self-awareness tends to be the most important foundation.

In the domain of self-awareness are three areas: emotional self-awareness, accurate self-assessment, and self-confidence. Let's see how these each relate to the other areas.

EMOTIONAL SELF-AWARENESS

The most basic skill of emotional intelligence is to know what you are feeling, right now, and be able to name it. When we first begin this journey, we are like people watching a parade. We just sit in one place and watch one thing after another move past us. When we are in this mode, we just observe our emotions moving past us. Perhaps they seem appropriate, and sometimes they just seem to be random. As we deepen the study, we learn that our emotions live in our body, each in a particular place, each with a particular sensation. They each have their own set of attachments to particular imprinting experiences that we have had in our life and to particular situations that we experience today. Most of us have the experience of a particular piece of music or style of music that evokes a consistent emotion, or a particular type of event that brings out the same feelings. There are countless examples of how this phenomenon is used to arouse patriotic spirit, as in flags flying, or hearing national anthems, or team spirit when hearing college fight songs. After experiencing the imprinting activities, the situation can arouse the same set of emotions consistently.

Once we learn this, we can actually use this as a skill. Rather than a random stream of emotions, we can see our emotional body like an ecosystem. Each emotion has its own home, its favorite trails through our consciousness, and a particular way that it can be called to come out and play. This is the level of emotional awareness we need to learn in order to be effective leaders of others' hearts. We have to first know our own heart.

One profound discovery of emotional awareness is how capable we are of actually changing our emotional state in moments. Emotions, by themselves, are brief and rapidly pass through our being. Our subconscious learns throughout our life to maintain emotions, creating complex moods and, when they become habitual, temperaments. It is a gift we give ourselves to learn that we are actually not slaves to emotion and that we can consciously choose how we would like to feel at a given time.

ACCURATE SELF-ASSESSMENT

This is an external validation piece that is required for us to get a good gauge on our emotional state and the impact that it has on others. Imagine that you sense a bit of agitation in yourself and identify that you feel a bit angry. A few minutes later, you find yourself cut off in traffic and subsequently shout out the window at the other driver, making gestures that indicate just how poor a driver he really is. Then, you pick up your coffee cup and notice your hand is shaking. You step out of your car and see that people are looking at you and slightly pulling away. Your phone rings, and you snap an answer: "What do you want?" If you were to step out of your being and observe that, would you say that you were a "bit angry"? Or would you say you were furious? Imagine that the next doorway you cross is into a meeting with your team. Are you set for leadership?

Sometimes, we have to arrange for feedback to get an external validation on how we come across or if the self-assessment we provide matches the reality that others experience. We can do this a number of ways, but it basically means that we get people we trust, who, in turn, trust us enough to provide an external set of feedback. Realize that their assessment will not necessarily be more accurate than our own and will be directly related to their training and skills in observation and removing their own personal judgment. However, it will be a gauge of sorts, through which we can understand our own emotions.

This is particularly significant in choosing the timing of engagements. It is best to know if we are actually furious, rather than just a bit angry. It is good to know if we are feeling a bit tired, or if we are really feeling sad and depressed. Our emotional state is as much of a message to the people around us as any business plan, financial presentation, or compelling opportunity. We must have the awareness of our emotions, coupled with an accurate yardstick to tell when and how much those emotions impact us. As leaders, however big the impact of our emotions are for us is how big the impact will be to our team.

SELF-CONFIDENCE

This one is just as it sounds—we need the emotional self-confidence that goes along with the mental clarity of direction. It is one thing for a person to give an intellectual run-down of the reasons that a plan will work, the associated risks, the mitigation strategies, and the potential rewards for taking that course. We can be confident in our plan, but what do we have to see or experience to believe that person is confident in herself? We can sense the fear in others, or the lack of confidence, or the egotistical ebullience of overconfidence bordering on cockiness.

There is a balance between these. Many visions require risk-taking and subsequent courage. Self-confidence does not mean complete fearlessness. It means the belief in yourself that you are up to the challenge, that you are ready, and that when problems occur, you will not shrink away in the moment.

Self-confidence is something that you build in yourself over time, by learning how to master your fears and knowing that you have been able to repeatedly keep yourself on course, get up when you have fallen, and try again when your plans have failed. You begin to build this experience base throughout your life.

While we often build self-confidence in various areas, such as athletic prowess or intellectual ability, it is common for some of us to have been very successful in many areas, while neglecting to build self-confidence in our ability to handle interpersonal issues. This is developed over time and through repeated action. While we might be completely confident that we can handle any business situation, we may have limited confidence in our ability to handle conflict or to support team members through tough times. This can be a recipe for avoidance or an overdependence on intellect and processes instead of on human contact. In order to lead, we must assess our level of confidence in our emotional resilience and power. If it is low, we must create situations to develop those skills.

BECOMING SELF-AWARE

Quite simply, this is turning our attention inward and knowing what it is that we are feeling. That is sometimes a bit more difficult than one might think, as we actually have many variations of emotions that can increase the complexity and often cloud our experience of a given situation. This is the ability to quickly sense our emotions, name them, and then take informed action based on the guidance offered through our emotional body.

This learning is based on the fact that our emotions existed before we had language and are not processed in the same way in which other information comes to us. Visual and auditory information comes to us through the associated parts of the brain and then is processed to create meaning. Through life, we have learned patterns and associations with this visual and auditory information and have developed a finely tuned ability to differentiate. This differentiation shows up in areas that are most important to us. For instance, we learn to differentiate food into groups, each of which we can readily identify—an apple, for example. If you like apples, you probably can identify different varieties of them, such as Fuji, Granny Smith, Golden Delicious, and McIntosh. There are many areas where we have developed a particular skill of discernment in an area that means something to us and helps us take meaningful action, based on the difference.

Our emotions, however, come to us through a different realm of perception that we learned prelanguage. They come as sensations and intuitions that are experienced and processed in the body and interpreted through the brain. Of particular relevance is that emotions impact our brain, whether we think we are listening to them or not. Additionally, most people have been trained, through years of education and socialization, to ignore much of the emotional data that they receive. We have to retrain our brains to use this emotional information, just as we use visual and auditory information. This can be challenging if we have been desensitized to our emotions. Many people tend to broadly characterize their emotions as angry, happy, or sad. While that is useful, it is like the broad categorization of food. We would not expect a chef to produce particularly appealing dishes if the best of his discernment was food or not food. By the same token, we would hardly expect a leader to orchestrate an emotionally moving engagement if all she could recognize was angry or happy.

All emotions have a basis in either love and trust or fear and doubt, so there is some value in this basic level of recognition. But to be more powerful, it is the more complex emotions that we want to learn to identify and manage. The better we can understand these emotions, the more we can do with regard to understanding others. It is impossible to empathize with someone to any degree of accuracy if we do not recognize the emotion in ourselves. A leader who recognizes that an organization is filled with a mixture of enthusiasm, trepidation, and ambiguity can connect with these emotions in such a way as to lead an emotional journey toward enthusiasm and optimism, simply by managing that journey within her own being, while being transparent and connected with the people involved. This is real leadership—using the power of self to clear the way for others to follow.

SPIRITUAL DEVELOPMENT FOR LEADERS

Here is the basis for inspiration: being inspired. People will only respond to you as deeply as you can be sensed. This is where you get personal power and the solidity of personality to create a compelling presence for those around you.

MINDFULNESS

Mindfulness is awareness of one's thoughts, actions, or motivations. There are many uses of this term, including the Buddhist meditation practice as a way of obtaining enlightenment. For our leadership practice, we focus on becoming aware of what we think about and when we think about it. People have the ability to expend their mental energy on the past, present, or future. Most people would agree that the only place they can truly live is in the present. While we often talk about or plan for the future, we can only get there through the now.

It is very important for leaders to connect with people in the now. When we sit down to talk to a person about what is going on for him, we must be able to stop the flow of thoughts and judgments that can fill our heads and focus purely on the person at hand. We know that people experience us through the limbic system, and they sense what is going on in us. Remember, too, that in a leadership position, people are more readily attuned to our system than we are to theirs. To provide the emotional safety and security for people to take great risks, we need to give them a solid place to go for support. This is done through our solid and connected emotional state, not through a series of random thoughts.

A friend of mine once described the experience of meeting Bill Clinton. It was in the middle of a large event, with thousands of people swarming everywhere. The Secret Service was surrounding then President Clinton as they moved through the vast group of people. People pushed in from all sides for a closer look or for a chance to exchange a word. My friend met the president on foot, in the center of an arena. She was struck for many years afterward with the feeling that she was the only person in the arena. She described his attention to her as "riveting," and that what she had to say was every bit as important as anything else that happened in that busy day—or any other day, for that matter. While the content faded away, the impression on her was long-lasting. In addition, her belief in his ability to lead went through the roof. From that point, she was completely committed to his vision. Whereas she had connected with it cognitively prior to that day, after that meeting she connected deeply with the person, which thoroughly cemented the bond.

While we strive to understand our emotions and be transparent and authentic, we must remain mindful that this understanding is like moving into a glass house. We become transparent, and people can see us. I once worked with a leader who made the statement, "Everyone knows exactly where I stand. If I'm mad, everyone knows it." What he did not realize was that he very often spent his time in journeys through the past and often harbored resentments and blame about events that had not turned out the way he thought they should. When he dealt with people around him, his thoughts rattled around in past decades, and his words would often come out inappropriately critical of the situation. Yes, everyone could see straight in, and what they saw was not pretty.

In order to evolve as a leader, he had to become mindful of what was in front of him in that particular moment. He had to recognize when his thoughts took him away from the moment and when his emotions were habits from the past, rather than responses to the present. In order to do this, he practiced ways of bringing himself into the moment and letting the banter of thoughts go away. He learned to let go of repetitive thoughts that took him out of the moment.

As he learned to quiet these old thoughts, he became aware of how much he had been missing in the moment. He realized that he had misunderstood many of the people who worked for him, as his mind was drifting much of the time. On the other side of this learning, the people around him became much calmer in his presence. They stopped fearing his anger, once they realized that he was going to actually listen to what they had to say through the ears of today, rather than through the recollection of yesterday.

COMPASSION

We have discussed the ability to empathize and its importance to leaders. In order to be an effective leader, it is imperative that we truly develop the ability to understand what people are feeling. Compassion is when we take that empathy to action and exercise an intention of making conditions better. Leaders take every opportunity to move toward a vision. This means that when we see people who are disenfranchised, who lack confidence, who are afraid, who are tired, or who are taken from their path for any reason, we will use our best energy to help them shift. In an organization or social context, this means that we help the ones who have made us angry or those we don't particularly like. We get to choose how we do this, but as leaders, living through inspirational presence, we are generous with the light of spirit that fuels us. It is an unlimited source, and overall, we can only benefit by this.

We extend compassion to the people who are working long hours and to our customers who use our services, as well as to those who chose not to. We extend compassion to our competitors. We extend compassion toward our environment and toward our planet. Once we begin expanding our awareness and learn the power of empathy, we will find countless ways to exercise compassion. It is vital to focus that energy on those who have chosen to take a journey with us. And through this compassion, people can learn to trust and depend upon us.

Most important, just as we have to learn to recognize our own feelings before we can experience empathy for others, we must learn to have compassion for ourselves—compassion for areas where our skills are less developed, rather than judging ourselves for a lack; compassion for ourselves when our plans fail, rather than considering ourselves a failure. It is through this exercise that we learn the art of compassion and the ability to apply it to others. It is through this that we can move away from habitual patterns of judgment and criticism. This allows us to liberate that energy to move toward higher causes and be used through our creativity and generativeness.

CONNECTING TO A HIGHER SOURCE

At some point, we all recognize that there is a higher consciousness than just our brain. Whatever we believe and however we choose to express it and practice it, we must have an internal guide that helps us elevate ourselves above the most basic parts of our humanity. Inspiration comes from the places of our highest consciousness, and this is done through a quietness of our inner being.

In order to lead, this inspiration needs to be the fuel for our being, not a badge that we wear. People recognize leaders who are deeply connected, as it comes through in the wisdom of their words, in the light in their eyes, and in the calmness of their voice. It is a source of strength, confidence, and comfort to leaders to understand this relationship between our humanity and our spirit.

HOW IT LOOKS IN ACTION— STORIES AND EXAMPLES

A senior leader in a very large global corporation spent many years working on his ability to connect with people through the use of himself. He used many parts of himself, including a love of music and songwriting, to connect with large groups.

As the corporation grew rapidly, his ability to work through any sort of control paradigm diminished exponentially. He recognized the need to lead through vision, and he crafted a metaphor and story about where he hoped to take his function. He told this story repeatedly, in setting after setting, crossing many cultural and ethnic boundaries. The story had relevance, but what really set the story apart was the story-teller.

During times of travel around the world, he focused on understanding the people at each location. He listened with deep attention, and he spoke from his heart about his convictions for what he was trying to do and why. During his times of reflection and introspection about what he was doing, his questions invariably turned to the appropriateness of what he was doing. Did it make a difference? Would the people who followed his lead benefit from this personally? Was his direction based on the highest good he could conceive? What did he hear from the people who had listened to him?

Through the course of this journey, the people who listened to him found many opportunities to move toward that goal immediately. They also created many long-term projects that were based on the vision in the story. Over the course of a few years, this global company found a series of interrelated processes that were all created to achieve the same vision.

He kept telling the story. Eventually, the story was told by others who were also trying to create the same change. Success increased, and the business flourished. He became known as a person of deep conviction, honesty, and integrity. People commented that they always knew where they stood with him, as he was known for his transparency of decision processes. He also developed the reputation of being hard on processes and strongly supportive of people. When mistakes were made, he sought to understand the events that led up to them and to help the people who made the mistakes to correct them and learn from them.

He became known for his presence. Most people recognized that it was not his energy of activity that created these processes, as all of them were larger by far than anything he could hope to do on his own. Rather, it was his energy of presence and being that inspired people to work together and create the vision he had started.

QUESTIONS TO ASK YOURSELF

Emotional Intelligence
- How well do I know myself emotionally?
- What sort of evidence do I have that I am correct?
- How do others see me?
  - An open book that they welcome reading?
  - A solid wall that has people guessing what is lurking behind it?
- Where do my thoughts live?
  - In the here and now?
  - In the there and then?
  - In the where and when?
- Do people welcome my support and guidance in times of turmoil or uncertainty?

Spiritual Development
- How often do I treat people around me with compassion?
  - With judgment?
  - With criticism?
- What do I believe about higher sources of knowledge and power?
- How willing am I to use that to guide my thoughts and actions?
- How open am I to sharing that with others?
- Am I willing to use myself to inspire others to success?

Exercise for Development

Go through the reading in this chapter and create a list of attributes of how you might behave if you exhibit them. Go to five people you trust, and ask them how they see you in these areas. Ask them for ways you could better live out these attributes. Take all of their feedback, and evaluate how you engage with others. Decide three things you will do to move into a place of higher effectiveness, and commit to them.

CHAPTER 10—LEADING GLOBALLY

If the success or failure of this planet and of human beings depended on how I am and what I do, how would I be? What would I do?

—Buckminster Fuller

In the 1990s we talked about what it took to work around the world, and we explored the cultural diversity and education required. For most of the people with whom I worked, it was a concept that seemed to be on the horizon. Most conversations centered on the issues of the difference of cultural norms and appropriate manners. We all learned how to properly exchange business cards in Asia, sit and eat properly in the Middle East, or negotiate in Russia. The book *Kiss, Bow or Shake Hands* (Morrison, Conway, and Boden, 1994) was on the required reading list. Now, most of my clients have the word global somewhere in their title or job description. Some have operations in well over one hundred countries. All will tell you that it takes far more than a basic understanding of etiquette and customs to create and sustain these global relationships. Most recognize that understanding the customs is important and moving gracefully in and out of these countries is definitely critical, but there is a basic aspect of humanity that needs additional focus.

Still, there are few consistent definitions of what it means to be a global leader. The most common and obvious issue expressed is that we are working 24/7, all around the world. It is an obviously pressing tactical issue to maintain ongoing operations on a global basis, but managing this most basic issue does little to guide a leader in how he works with his global organization. At its worst, a global organization throws off circadian rhythms, as some work from four in the morning until midnight, trying to manage in the same ways they did when their organization was in fewer time zones—or even just on the same hallway. The number of different holidays observed by their workforce fills their calendars, and they spend an unnecessary amount of time scheduling phone conversations. A planning consideration becomes how to effectively use thirty-hour trips halfway around the world.

It is one thing to prepare for a business trip to another country to negotiate a contract or find local support for a project; this can be planned and has a beginning, middle, and an end for the leader. Altogether different is the global structure of an ongoing operation with direct reports in different countries, all of whom are of different nationalities and trying to create a common end. The ability to control and be physically connected drops exponentially in these cases. Now, we work vastly by influence and by communications mediums of reduced effectiveness, such as phone calls and emails. It seems that these issues can cloud the larger issue at hand that occurs through these business relationships.

Quite simply, the global business climate is opening a portal into new possibilities for overall global relationships. The way in which these multi-national and global companies operate actually establishes cultural relationships more quickly than has happened through political actions and alliances. These relationships create great change around the world, as well as serving to redistribute wealth and influence. The fabric of these agreements can serve us globally—or not. It is incumbent on leaders of today to look beyond the immediate implications and imagine what the best results can be for our world. We can live in an "and" world, and accomplish business objectives and have everyone ultimately win. It falls to our new generation of transformational leaders to create these conditions. One further caveat here: I am talking about leaders who lead globally, not just leaders of global enterprises.

OPERATING GLOBALLY

One thing is very clear to anyone who has done any sort of global work. The bigger implications of global leadership lie in the cross-cultural nature of the work. We deal with people who have significantly different filters of the world. Due to the inherent nature of perception, the world that they see has many different aspects. Remember that we work with people who speak different languages (meaning there is a different representational system of the world), pray to different gods, and have different economic value systems—these are just some of the big ones. We also know that in most cross-cultural situations, it is usually not the big differences that can become problems but the small ones, which go somewhat unnoticed.

Some anthropologists assert that translation from one language to another is actually not possible. While we can convert the words from one representation into another one, we choose a word that is a representation of an experience within one environment and culture, and then choose a rough equivalent that is actually a representation of another experience within a different environment and culture. While the experience may be similar, it is not the same as the experience through the other culture. It is a realization that we need to engage as we begin our exploration into global leadership. We need to take this as a way of opening our eyes to limits in our existing perspective, not as a limitation of what is possible for us to learn. We can gain deep knowledge and appreciation of different cultures through experiencing them. The skills pertinent to global leadership are not necessarily to develop a deep understanding of a large number of cultures—although that certainly wouldn't hurt—but to learn *how* to understand cultures. A global leader will operate from a perspective of being open to the adventure of the difference.

ESTABLISHING RAPPORT

It is essential for the global leader to understand how to enter and build rapport and to use this skill to expand his empathic abilities. Developing emotional intelligence is a real key to crossing cultural boundaries. While our brains may speak a different language, our limbic systems do not. The basic emotions of love, fear, disgust, and anger are recognized—across cultures—through facial expressions. We know that the same emotions are felt, lived, enjoyed, and tolerated globally, but the meaning-making system that is used by every human is culturally specific and has been built into his or her environment. Consequently, even though we can decode some of the nuances of culture, we can never decode the experience of that culture. Instead, we have to create a symbolic representation of that cultural experience by opening ourselves empathically. The global leader will learn to connect with the humanity of the people she is leading.

Learning cultural mannerisms and greetings is a great first step to establishing rapport. It is not, however, the entire method. Imagine that you meet someone of a different nationality, who has taken the time to learn an initial greeting in your language. Your first reaction is that the person has moved the engagement to meet you on your ground. As soon as that exchange passes, however, he communicates with you in his native language, which you do not understand at all. He continues to talk at you and grows increasingly agitated at your lack of response.

In this example, the person learned a greeting but did not enter into empathic rapport with you. While this may be a bit extreme, it is much like something I have witnessed among people who start their work across cultural lines. The most basic awareness is that there is a very real difference in the experience of the world, and we need to open with the willingness to see, listen, and feel what others are experiencing through our contact.

CURIOSITY

One incredibly simple technique of building cultural sensitivity is to practice being curious. Just look at each situation and wonder, with childlike sincerity, what is going on there. Try to understand things from the perspective of what it is like for the other person, rather than how you will use the information. Imagine yourself in his situation, in his culture, and try to get a feeling for what his experience is like. Ask genuine and sincere questions that are intended to build understanding and create relationships.

DECISION STRATEGIES

Every person has a unique way of making decisions. Even among groups that are relatively homogenous culturally, making decisions can be a concern or even cause significant problems. There are often large differences in people with regard to whether they make decisions based on facts and data or based on feelings and intuitions. This can be a big issue for leaders. When we include cultural differences, we add many more wrinkles to this equation. The very large categories of differences still exist, but they are now multiplied by the addition of different cultural interpretations to each area.

The good news is that we can understand decision strategies and the subsequent differences in anyone, and then we can generalize our techniques into cross-cultural situations. Once we master these, the process will serve us universally. Here are some things that we need to consider about decision making:

- Understand what people see as data. Is it facts and figures? Sensory experience? Stories told by people who matter to them? Once you find out what a person is looking for, you can work to find the proper way to represent the situation. This is a big difference in corporate settings, when the difference is caused by functional training. Accountants view data differently than do scientists. When you add on the cultural differences presented through a global operation, the differences can become extreme.
- Understand the deliberation process. Some people need quiet time to decide. Others need to verbalize and try out their decisions. Some people need to have a trial decision posed to them and respond to it. However they work, see if you can step into that experience and relate to what it is like for them. Talk to them about how they process things, and then try it for yourself. You might actually find something that works better than what you have used before.

APPROACH TO AUTHORITY

Remember, authority means something different to each of us. When you add on a cultural context, we often cannot even understand the difference in authority between natives of, for instance, Africa, China, Japan, Venezuela, and the United States. Even when we see it and notice it, we still interpret the other person's difference through our own experience. Again, we need to recognize that these differences are very significant and be conscious about how we are either working with this or against it. The only way we can realize it is to become experimental and curious about people's motivational factors. We can learn to be sensitive to these differences and then enroll people to help us understand.

BUILDING COMMUNITIES
OF GLOBAL COLLABORATION

It was the mid-70s, I was eighteen and still thanking Richard Nixon the first thing every morning for ending the draft just in time for me to avoid a free trip to Vietnam. Most of my friends and relatives were back from their tours there, with the final withdrawals imminent. Growing up with a decade of conflict in the nightly news had the issues of war and peace fresh on my mind, as well as on the minds of most of the people with whom I was attending university. We were in a sociology class when someone asked the professor, "What would it take to create world peace?" His answer, at the time, seemed laughable. It was simply: "Alien invasion. That is the only thing that could bring the entire world together."

Today, that makes more sense to me from a perspective of boundary differences, although the argument still falls apart at the end. He simply meant that if there was a force that created a boundary big enough to include the entire world, we would unify against it. Alien invasion implies that there is still war, only now it is not just between us humans. We would all fight on the same side against whatever force was coming in. We've seen this in cinema such as *Independence Day*, or maybe we've read *The War of the Worlds*. There is another presupposition in this statement—only through threat could humans be unified. I believe that it is an equally valid proposition that humans could be unified through aspiration and that there are ideals that would be universally compelling to humans, regardless of nationality.

Today, I see a little farther out. I can agree that a force that is large enough to create a boundary around the entire world could have the effect of creating global unification. I also believe these forces exist. An example is the environment. There is only one, and it bounds and nourishes us all equally. We are quickly learning that the earth is very small and very connected when it comes to receiving our actions. This global connection is teaching us that we are highly interdependent in terms of life on this planet, and we cannot truly succeed if the by-product of that success creates great harm to others. There can never be a genuine success that results in harm to some.

One aspect of leadership at a global level is an understanding of the larger system implications of our actions. Corporate leaders have as much impact across countries as our political systems, and in many cases, far more. How will you develop the large system sensitivity to understand the economic, social, and environmental implications of the work you do at a global level?

We must find our positive global intention that we can carry with us when we plan our global activities. We can talk to many people to understand what our impact is from multiple perspectives. We can create communities of awareness that have, at their core, a desire for positive change in the world at a global level.

Because of the size and scope of the potential impacts and subsequent changes of our actions, it is probably impossible for one person to imagine the overall consequences. This is further limited by the fact that individually, we make all of our predictions based on our unique worldview, filled with our own cultural experience. We can only hope to create groups of people who can co-create communities that will collectively come up with global implications of actions. At this point, we are working to establish groups of people who basically function as peers, common as citizens of the world, who want the same things and who hold the same vision. The challenge as a global leader is to hold the multiple interests at heart and see the possibilities of how groups of people, who are seemingly very different, can work together to accomplish an overall higher goal.

AVOIDING COLONIALISM

History shows many accounts of various nations that have expanded their boundaries into the territories of other countries. Sometimes these intrusions were hostile—countries sought to gain control of resources. Other times, they have been friendlier and had more reciprocal agreements. You will see, though, that consistently, any nation that established a presence for the purpose of exploiting a resource (even if it seemed benevolent) eventually lost the benefit of the relationship. Eventually, people will respond equivalently to the level of equity in any relationship. If that relationship begins in a dependant and inequitable fashion, eventually the dependant party will develop to the point of demanding something different.

In many corporate settings, business units set up across multiple nationalities and, very often, in developing countries. Some of these companies function quite differently in the environment of other countries than in their home country. Those companies that have developed a global consciousness will apply the same value set of people and environment everywhere they go, because it is the right thing to do. Other companies will exploit low-cost labor or less stringent environmental protection laws in the interest of profit. This short-termed thinking can produce temporary benefits, but it will ultimately go the same direction as the various colonialist movements in our human history.

Now, saying that a company applies a consistent value set globally does not mean that it exports its own culture. It means there is a deeper set of values around the worth of the people with whom it does business, and there is an expectation of reciprocity. We must look at the overall implications of success at much larger levels than those that serve our own immediate gain.

There is a basic rule in general systems theory: whenever we optimize a sub-part of a system, we consequently sub-optimize the larger system, unless all of the optimization intentions are consistent across the different levels. This said, if we think about the world as one of the larger levels of system, and there are sub-systems within that (countries), whenever we optimize a country's agenda without consideration for aligned intention at a global level, we necessarily sub-optimize the larger system or the world. This is particularly true when we add competition, which has the explicit goal of optimizing at another sub-system's expense. It has a component of win/lose.

In order to reach the optimal solution, we must begin with a desire for the ultimate win/win. This allows us to step beyond the immediate goals that we are trying to accomplish and look at the situation from a much larger perspective. We must literally step out of our ordinary self and see the situation from the largest possible perspective. Einstein put forward some of the great advances in quantum physics through the use of thought experiments, in which he would imagine the "what if" of a concept. He would take those concepts and try to imagine them on the largest possible scope, in which he began to see new possibilities, validation of concepts, or places where the concepts fell apart. This is what we must learn to do as global leaders—imagine things happening on a scale that is larger than we ever dreamed possible, with benefits for all of us that are greater than have ever been seen before.

THINK GLOBALLY, ACT LOCALLY

Global leadership does not necessarily have to mean leading a global enterprise. We can each lead on a global level if we think of the global implications of every action we take. I have tried to stress this distinction and that we need leaders of every sort, in every walk of life, who have taken on the idea of thinking through their actions to a level of global impact. This is the base power of transformational leadership. Many executives who rise to a level where they have global organizations are often caught with the same struggle of "How do I lead globally?" The individual transformation is just one of perspective and alignment. It is learning to start with a global perspective and aligning our actions with it.

Let us take the challenge to do this one simple thing. It is an old saying, but it is perpetually appropriate: Think globally, and act locally. This is something we can do in every aspect of our life, and it becomes a discipline. The term *globally* can be thought of as a larger level of system, and we can learn to align actions across multiple levels of system. This might mean that I think about my own actions, how they will impact my work group or my office, and how that will impact the company direction. Are they in alignment? We look for a consistent directive correlation, so that an improvement in one area translates into improvements in all areas.

This is a key skill area for executives who have reached the level of organizational responsibility where they are looking for enterprise impact of individual actions. When we think of large systems, we can never really know how impacts will play out, but we can imagine. We can create hypotheses, which then will lead us to informed and conscious action.

Wherever you are, whatever you are doing, take responsibility for your actions at the largest possible level. Think about the global impacts of what you are doing or not doing. Find some issue in the world that you truly care about and begin considering the impact of your every action (or inaction) related to that issue.

HOW IT LOOKS IN ACTION

Consider the story of Jeremy Gilley. At age twenty-nine, this British film-maker set off with a camera and the fundamental belief that the media had the social responsibility of promoting peace. His mission: establish one day of peace a year, a global cease-fire honored annually. His logic was simple. If we can do it for one day, then maybe we will learn how to do it every day. His documentary of the process, *Peace One Day*, shows how he was able to speak to an astounding number of heads of state, non-governmental organizations (NGOs), United Nations leaders, and Nobel Peace Prize laureates, as well as students, activists, and celebrities. After five years, thousands of letters, tens of thousands of miles of travel, and countless meetings, he won the sponsorship of the United Kingdom and Costa Rican governments to put forth a proposition in the United Nations, which passed unanimously (UN GA A/Res/55/282) and created September 21 as a global cease-fire and day of nonviolence. He is absolute proof that committed individuals can make a global difference.

Jeremy did not accomplish this through one big transformation. He accomplished thousands upon thousands of microtransformations among the people he engaged. He did not accomplish this through proposing policies or practices to the heads of state, as might have been done in political negations. He appealed to the hearts of people who cared about their own countries as well as the world. He carried a vision, clear and succinct, that people around the world could appreciate equally. That is the essence of living through inspiration and leading transformation through the hearts and minds of committed people. He held a vision, he set goals, he enrolled many diverse groups of people—many of whom worked in teams—and he took action on his vision through his life and his work. His vision opened doors, and his passion carried his message.

If Jeremy can do it, so can I. So can you. So can any one of us or all of us. The question is quite simple: What is it that you will do? What are the larger outcomes with which you align your thoughts and actions? What is the greater good that you will put at least part of your energy toward? If not you, then who? If not now, then when?

QUESTIONS TO ASK YOURSELF

- What global issues matter to me?
- To what extent do I believe that they matter to others?
- How does my lifestyle impact those global issues? (Head's up—there is no "not at all" answer here.)
- What do I do now that makes a positive impact on this global issue?
  - How can I make that impact bigger?
  - How can I enroll more people to have a similar impact?
- Am I making a difference today in a way that is most reflective of the highest part of me?
- Have I put my heart into my work today?
- If 10,000 people were doing the same things that I did today, would the world improve more quickly? What if it was 100,000? A million?
- If I could instantly have the resources to have one million people all simultaneously take some action that I believe would most further an important cause, what would it be?
  - Am I taking that action myself? Can I?

CONCLUSION—MAKING IT REAL

As our circle of knowledge expands, so does the circumference of darkness surrounding it.

—Albert Einstein

Now we come to the point of making it all real. The preceding chapters have presented a number of concepts and models, as well as questions intended to make the content more relevant and personal. At this point, you have the choice as to what you do with what you have read. All of this is only relevant to the degree you manifest it and create transformation through your life.

We never really know how much we can accomplish, particularly when we take the approach of microtransformations. One of the interesting things about transformation of our thoughts is that the moment we step into a different way of seeing the world, everything else around us shifts. The larger we set our sights, the more new mysteries appear. Each offers the opportunity for new learning and new accomplishments. Each of the areas we have discussed here can be learned and perfected, simply through practice and intention. We can do some specific things to develop in each of the areas, so here are some tips:

SEE YOURSELF CLEARLY

One of the first things I do when I work with a leader is help him to see himself as clearly as possible. This involves assessing him against a number of instruments that give him general information about his personality, his approach to conflict, and his orientation to groups. Additionally, I get specific information from many people who know that leader's behavior and style. This exercise of getting feedback can be absolutely mind-blowing to some people, depending on how differently they see themselves from how others see them.

Every person develops a different process for his preferred orientation to the world, whether he spends his time focused on others, himself, ideas, or whatever. Very often the picture we create of ourselves has a great deal of distortion in it. There is always some, so the idea is to refine that image so that we have a good idea of the way in which we think we put out is actually seen by others.

This is best done through a number of channels and by measuring a number of dimensions. I believe it is most important to get clear behavioral data through stories and specific examples, as we have to remember that the way others see us has its unique distortion as well. We often say that feedback tells us as much about the person giving it as the person receiving it. However, this is not an excuse to dismiss it; it's just a reason to get multiple sources and look for trends or themes.

During the course of learning about yourself, try to understand how you look in action with the world. Many of us have never seen our facial reactions during conversations or how we look when we are fearful or angry. Get videotaped as you deliver key messages—that is a powerful way for you to observe what others see. Find out how expressive you are. Find out how your voice sounds.

Also, understand your decision-making style. This has been a key area of focus for most of my clients over my years in this work. There are many different ways that each of us arrives at key decisions and how we are convinced that we have gotten enough information. This can make a huge difference among groups, and it's a key issue for anyone leading others. You must know enough about yourself to be clear in groups and know enough about others' styles to ensure that they are getting what they need as well.

This is a good place to get some help. Find someone who is trained in questioning and observation processes to help you get meaningful information. Also, be sure to set up a support group for afterward, as you might have to spend some time processing what you have heard. Talking to trusted people can be valuable.

The last step of learning about yourself is to decide what to do with the information. Remember the concept of microtransformation: simply picking one thing to consistently notice will produce change by itself.

Most important, change things about yourself because those things are important for who you want to be, not because others want you to change. Look for information that will help you know and understand yourself, not instructions of how others want you to be.

CHANGE YOUR MIND

The simplest aspect of change is to simply change your mind. I don't mean this lightly—truly change the way you see the world and challenge your core beliefs. Our belief sets drive many of our experiences of the world, not only through what meaning we make of our experience but also in that our beliefs drive the questions we ask and the experiences that we seek.

Brain research in the past decades has given us proof of the renewability of the brain. Where it was once thought that our brain did not change throughout our adult life, we now know about neuroplasticity, or the malleable quality of the brain. There are 10,000 new neural networks formed every day. The brain is very willing to create these networks in new configurations, if you simply "ask" it to do so. Without input, the brain creates replacements for old networks and basically recreates itself in the image of what has been important in the past.

However, if you go through the mental exercises, changing your perceptions, you will recreate your brain in new configurations on a daily basis. Every time you get an "aha" experience, you have rewired some portion of your brain. This microtransformation creates a new pathway through which any information is processed and will give new perception on old experiences.

One of the most effective ways to accomplish these changes is through neurolinguistic programming (NLP). You can learn incredibly simple practices to reframe experiences and shift your emotional states. When we repeatedly shift states, we produce trait changes. This is ultimately what is desired—to create a practice of seeing the world through our most resourceful states.

DEVELOP AN ENVISION PRACTICE

Take the time to identify your practice. Ask any serious musician, artist, dancer, martial artist, or actor about his or her practice. He will tell you what it is. As a leader, you are your product, so your practice must be holistic and include all parts that others will engage. Think of how you would create a practice that includes body, mind, emotion, spirit, and your particular movements to action. Base this on improvements you'd like to make in yourself—ideally, based on what you learned from seeing yourself in the light of leadership.

Most of the people with whom I have worked, many in senior leadership roles, previously had spent very little time thinking about how they could become better at their ability to lead. Most spent their time thinking about how to get others to do what they wanted in a very transactional style. One of the first things they had to do was to adopt practices designed to increase their ability to lead.

There are simple things to do: adopting a practice of goal setting and regular affirmations is one. This will allow to shape your mental images and your self-talk. Also, adopt a practice of being mindful and managing your thoughts. Mediation is one way to do that. Remember that your physicality is deeply involved in your leadership, so create a practice that can strengthen your body, such as yoga or Pilates, which gives you more stamina as well as a better ability to think clearly. Anything that keeps you aware of how you are using your body will make a positive impact. On top of that, it is much easier to be positive and optimistic when you feel better. Whatever practice you choose, make it one that you love, that is distinctly your own, and that is intended to serve your highest good.

Why don't you take a moment right now and think about how you will practice being a leader. Write it down.

COMMIT TO CHANGE

This is a time to commit to change. It is one thing to read a book and learn concepts or identify new techniques. In order to make any of it matter, you must first commit to change. Remember that you will need to anchor this commitment, just as a vision, and ensure that you have disconnected from anything that may no longer serve you on this road. Until we commit our energy and our thoughts, nothing ever happens. We must find that direction and start taking steps. Even if it is only one thing, we start.

One very quick and effective anchor is to publicly state what you are going to do. Here's a way to do that:

- Take a moment and review what you have read and learned in the course of this book.
- Find the most compelling thing you can commit to immediately that will allow you to build your inspirational presence.
- Write it up and email it to me at commitments@inspirationalpresence.com. I'd like to see it.

Do it now. Decide. Change your mind. Replan your day, your week, your life. Go inside and find your passion, then go out and set the world on fire with it.

BONUS OFFER

Bonus offer for readers of *Inspirational Presence*.

$79 video of Dr. Jeff Evans as he presents leadership case studies. These stories describe leaders who have used their presence to create inspiration and transformation.

This video gives you another method of learning these vital skills and developing your own Inspirational Presence. In addition to the content provided, you will find other bonus offers presented during the course of the video.

Claim your training video now.

Go to http://inspirationalpresence.com/bonus.htm and download it for free.

ABOUT THE AUTHOR

Jeff Evans, Ph.D., is a leadership development consultant, executive coach, author, and speaker. He is the founder and owner of the Gaian Group, a leadership development firm. His work focuses on developing and supporting dynamic, inspirational presence in leaders. He has spent the past 20 years supporting executives through transformational change. During this time, Jeff has consulted to leaders of some of the largest corporations in the world, many of whom lead global organizations spanning over 100 counties. He has also consulted on new organization designs and startups, large group change methodologies, and joint ventures and alliances in international and global settings. His client base has ranged from international executive teams to manufacturing management teams in retail, manufacturing, information technology, telecommunications, research and development, as well as oil and gas exploration.

Jeff is co-author of the book *Ten Tasks Of Change* (Jossey/Bass-Pfeiffer, 2001), as well as numerous papers and research studies on learning organizations, leadership, training design, and training systems. He has developed and taught extension courses through UC Berkeley's College of Business in Systems Thinking, Managing Change, and Consulting Skills.

Jeff has been a key presenter at numerous conferences in the areas of leadership or change, organization development, and large-scale change methodologies. He has undergraduate and graduate degrees in education and social sciences, including a Ph.D. in Educational Human Resource Development from Texas A&M. He completed a 3 Year Post-Graduate track in organization development at the Gestalt Institute in Cleveland and has done post-doctoral work in behavioral systems, organizations, the psychology of group dynamics, and emotional intelligence. He is also a Certified Hypnotherapist and a Master Practitioner in NeuroLinguistic Programming (NLP).

PRAISE FOR INSPIRATIONAL PRESENCE

A fine blend of theory and practice, the book masterfully weaves leadership, emotional intelligence and systems thinking into a highly useful guide for anyone who has ever truly wished to make a difference; in their life, their organization, their community or world. It's destined to become a great piece of work of this decade.

Todd H. Slingsby - Vice President of People & Organization Development The Clorox Company

"Jeff explores the mystery that there is inherent structure that prevents a person from taking steps toward his or her vision. He gives compelling examples and steps to help leaders work in transformational ways during thee challenging times."

Rick Maurer - author Beyond the Wall of Resistance

"Inspirational Presence, The Art of Transformational Leadership is timely and relevant at a time when organizations are desperately looking for ways to adapt and survive. Jeff Evans offers an essential roadmap to navigate in the new globally interconnected world, by deeply probing into the higher ground that defines and guides the successful leader and organization."

Mark B. Glick/Director of Economic Development/Office of Hawaiian Affairs

This thoughtful and well-written book provides a very useful guide to people in leadership positions of all kinds, and at all levels. Jeff Evans has done a great job of synthesizing theory and practice.

Edwin C. Nevis, Ph.D.- Co-Founder, Gestalt International Study Center

As he accomplished in his earlier book, *Ten Tasks of Change,* Jeff demystifies another topic: leadership. In *Inspirational Presence,* each chapter offers you an opportunity to explore a critical aspect of leadership in global settings. The "Questions to Ask Yourself" at the end of each chapter are a practical tool to help you face your own reality. Drawing upon the work of other leaders in the field, Jeff presents a compelling, well-defined, and practical approach to leading globally.

Elaine Biech - Author & Consultant

Jeff Evans looks well beyond the tools, processes and behaviors of leadership to the deepest roots of the spirit of leadership... of truly <u>being</u> a leader in ones heart and soul. He taps into the elements of human nature and psychology common to all cultures past and present to arrive at the *essence* of a state of mind of transformational leadership that can enable each of us to accomplish great things. I highly recommend this book!

Gilles (Jeal) A. Eberhard - General Manager, Strategy and Planning - Chevron Corporation

This book is a must read for anyone interested in supporting transformational change across multiple levels of system and accessing one's indwelling intelligence as an aspect of self mastery. Jeff has managed to articulate in writing the most cutting edge thinking and practice in the field.

John D. Carter Ph.D. - Gestalt OSD Center, President

It is an art of inspiration for the leaders and the management students to adapt their style according to the changed globalized world of our epoch.

Dr. Liz Thach - Professor of Management and Wine Business - Sonoma State University

Inspirational Presence is a valuable book on an important topic. It is based on a wide mix of research, sprinkled with real life experiences and is guaranteed to expand your perspective, and if you apply it's lessons, make a difference in your life and the lives you lead. Highly recommended!

Kevin Eikenberry, author Remarkable Leadership, Unleashing Your Leadership Potential One Skill at a Time.

These extraordinary and evolutionary times call for expanded and evolutionary thinking. The methods used by the leaders of yesterday will not suffice in this new world. Inspirational Presence provides powerful and innovative ideas, as well as life-changing tools for the leaders of the future.

Pamala Oslie - Author of Life Colors, Love Colors, & Make Your Dreams Come True

If you want to change your company, first change yourself. Only when the leader is open to new and better things can those around him or her catch that vibe, that inspiration and move with their rhythm.

Ken Knowles - Program Manager, Information Management Transformation Chevron Information Technology Company

"This work is an interesting, thought-provoking, and practical guide that demystifies the art and science of being an inspirational leader. Anyone can easily read this book in one sitting as it tells how to become a transformational leader in simple easy to follow steps. The journey to self awareness, and personal power is worth the effort. This is one book in your collection that will be dog eared and underlined."

Adrienne Seal - Sr. Organization Development Mgr The Clorox Company and co-founder Spirit Tree consulting (a coaching and consulting practice)

Why just motivate your people when you can inspire them? With this book, Jeff has given us a very clear blueprint for how to become that leader that inspires positive change and creates a vision others will want to follow...

Brian Dutter, M.B.A., Entreprenuer

BIBLIOGRAPHY

Bion, Winifred R. *Experiences in Groups*. New York: Ballantine Books, 1975.

Canfield, Jack and Janet Schwitzer. *The Success Principles*. New York: Collins, 2007.

Covey, Steven. *The 7 Habits of Highly Effective People*. New York: Simon & Schuster, 1990.

Evans, Jeff and Chuck Schaefer. *Ten Tasks of Change; Demystifying Changing Organization*. San Francisco: Jossey/Bass–Pfeiffer, 2001.

Goleman, **Daniel**, Richard Boyatzi, and Annie McKee. *Primal Leadership. **Realizing** the Power of Emotional Intelligence*. Boston: Harvard **Business** School Press, 2001.

Goleman, **Daniel**. *Emotional Intelligence. Why it can matter more than IQ*. **New** York: Bantam Books, 1997.

H.H. Dali Lama. *The Art of Happiness: A Handbook for Living*. New York: Riverwood Hardcover, 1998.

Kouzes, James, and Barry Posner. *The Leadership Challenge*. San Francisco: Jossey/Bass, 2007.

MacTaggert, Lynn. *The Field; The Quest for the Secret Force of the Universe*. New York: Harper, 2008.

MacTaggert, Lynn. *The Intention Experiment; Using your Thoughts to Change Your Life and the World*. New York: Free Press, 2008.

Machiavelli, Niccolo. *The Prince*. Boston: Dante University of America Press, 2003.

Miguel, Don Ruiz. *The Four Agreements*. San Rafael: Amber-Allen Publishing, 1997.

Morrison, Terri, Wayne Conaway, and George Borden. *Kiss, Bow or Shake Hands*. Darby: Diane Publishing Co, 1994.

Perls, Fritz. *The Gestalt Approach and Eye Witness to Therapy*. Palo Alto: Science and Behaviors Books, 1973.

Peter, Laurence and Raymond Hull. *The Peter Principle*. New York: William Morrow & Co., 1969.

Senge, Peter. *The Fifth Discipline*. New York: Doubleday Business, 1994.

Tzu, Sun. *The Art of War*. Boston: Shambala, 2005.

Weber, Max. *Economy and Society*. Berkeley: University of California Press, 1978.

Wells, H. G. *The War of the Worlds*. New York: A Tor Book, 1988.

Wilbur, Ken. *The Marriage of Sense and Soul*. New York: Broadway Books, 1998.

Wilbur, Ken. *A Brief History of Everything*. Boston: Shambala, 1996.

Williamson, MaryAnn. *Return to Love*. New York: HarperCollins, 1993.

Zuchav, Gary. *Heart of the Soul*. New York: Simon & Schuster, 2001.

Zuchav, Gary. *The Dancing Wu Li Masters; An Overview of the New Physics*. New York: William Morrow, 1979.

BUY A SHARE OF THE FUTURE IN YOUR COMMUNITY

These certificates make great holiday, graduation and birthday gifts that can be personalized with the recipient's name. The cost of one S.H.A.R.E. or one square foot is $54.17. The personalized certificate is suitable for framing and will state the number of shares purchased and the amount of each share, as well as the recipient's name. The home that you participate in "building" will last for many years and will continue to grow in value.

THIS CERTIFIES THAT

YOUR NAME HERE

HAS INVESTED IN A HOME FOR A DESERVING FAMILY

1985-2005

TWENTY YEARS OF BUILDING FUTURES IN OUR COMMUNITY ONE HOME AT A TIME

1200 SQUARE FOOT HOUSE @ $65,000 = $54.17 PER SQUARE FOOT
This certificate represents a tax deductible donation. It has no cash value.

Here is a sample SHARE certificate:

YES, I WOULD LIKE TO HELP!

I support the work that Habitat for Humanity does and I want to be part of the excitement! As a donor, I will receive periodic updates on your construction activities but, more importantly, I know my gift will help a family in our community realize the dream of homeownership. **I would like to SHARE in your efforts against substandard housing in my community!** *(Please print below)*

PLEASE SEND ME _____ SHARES at $54.17 EACH = $ $_____

In Honor Of: _____

Occasion: (Circle One)   HOLIDAY   BIRTHDAY   ANNIVERSARY

OTHER: _____

Address of Recipient: _____

Gift From: _____ *Donor Address:* _____

Donor Email: _____

I AM ENCLOSING A CHECK FOR $ $_____ PAYABLE TO HABITAT FOR HUMANITY <u>OR</u> PLEASE CHARGE MY VISA OR MASTERCARD *(CIRCLE ONE)*

Card Number _____ Expiration Date: _____

Name as it appears on Credit Card _____ Charge Amount $ _____

Signature _____

Billing Address _____

Telephone # Day _____ Eve _____

PLEASE NOTE: Your contribution is tax-deductible to the fullest extent allowed by law.
Habitat for Humanity • P.O. Box 1443 • Newport News, VA 23601 • 757-596-5553
www.HelpHabitatforHumanity.org

LaVergne, TN USA
19 November 2009
164628LV00002B/124/P